Colombia and the United States

Colombia and the United States
War, Unrest, and Destabilization

Mario A. Murillo

with Jesus Rey Avirama

An Open Media Book

SEVEN STORIES PRESS
New York

In Canada:
Hushion House, 36 Northline Road, Toronto, Ontario M4B 3E2

In the U.K.:
Turnaround Publisher Services Ltd., Unit 3,
Olympia Trading Estate, Coburg Road, Wood Green,
London N22 6TZ

In Australia:
Palgrave Macmillan, 627 Chapel Street, South Yarra, VIC 3141

Cover design: Greg Ruggiero

Cover image: A Colombian soldier searches a man for a firearm March 10, 2002, in Bogotá, Colombia. The man being frisked is assisting voters in the election for senators and congressmen. The search is to ensure that the voting process is not interrupted or influenced in any way. The elections were surprisingly very calm and peaceful despite boycott threats by the Revolutionary Armed Forces of Colombia (FARC). (Photo by Carlos Villalon/Getty Images)

Map of Colombia: Amelia Janes, © 2003 by Midwest Educational Graphics

ISBN 1-58322-606-0

Printed in Canada.

9 8 7 6 5 4 3 2 1

For Kerabania and Nemo, whose energy, curiosity, and intelligence provide the fuel for my optimism that there is hope for the future.

Contents

Acknowledgments

Trying to make sense of the situation in Colombia is not an easy task, given its history of unrest and contradiction, not to mention the constantly shifting contemporary social and political crisis. This book is really the product of my own evolutionary perspective on the internal conflict, undoubtedly shaped by many personal experiences in the country my father calls home. From the outset, I think it is important to point out that my frame of reference is from a physical distance, despite spending almost every summer traveling throughout Colombia, visiting regularly with my family since I was an infant, and having lived in Bogotá for a couple of years in the early 1980s. Yes, I maintain a deep emotional proximity to Colombia, with family and professional ties forever linking me to it. But I say this with considerable humility, understanding that many of the judgments and observations made in these pages may indeed reflect the comfort of someone who has not had to live the horrors of the decades-long conflict on a daily basis. Having the luxury of completing the book in Colombia has driven this point home for me even further. Regardless of how much I've tried to remain on top of the situation from afar, there is nothing like feeling the pulse of Colombia on a daily basis, exchanging ideas with everybody from the ice cream vendor on the corner to the city's many taxi drivers, from the human rights activists and journalists to the dozens of young people I'm in touch with in different parts of the country.

For the most part, the thoughts expressed herein are based on hundreds of interviews and conversations I have had over the years with people from all political stripes and perspectives, both within and outside of Colombia. Some of my general observations, therefore, can be interpreted as summaries of this large collection of interviews and conversations. My perspective on Colombia is also based on watching the "Colombia story" unfold in the U.S. and Colombian media, gems and distortions alike, as well as the dozens of books, journals, and articles written by both Colombian and foreign writers about myriad issues relating to Colombian history, culture, and politics. Over the past fifteen years I have been able to transform many of these experiences and exchanges into media reports, written and produced for both radio and print. Throughout this time I have had the fortune of meeting many dynamic, committed, and talented people, all of whom have left quite an impression on me. In essence, the thoughts enclosed here are meant to be a synthesis of all these sources, which is why it would be impossible for me to acknowledge all those who may have had a hand in its completion.

The actual book, however, is a collaboration with someone I consider to be a close friend and comrade, a mentor, and an astute political analyst—Jesus Rey "Chucho" Avirama—whom I first met in 1992 during a visit to Cauca, Colombia. I was familiar with Chucho's long history of activism within the indigenous movement in Colombia, given that he was one of the founders of the Regional Indigenous Council of Cauca (CRIC), and a veteran national and international spokesperson for various indigenous struggles. I admired the dedication and selfless commitment he and his brothers in the movement had toward questions of social justice and peace, not only for their immediate Kokonuco community, but also for indigenous, peasant, poor, and working people in general throughout Colombia. Over the years I have gotten to know Chucho on many levels—from his sharp wit and sinister sense of humor, to his critical perspective on U.S. foreign and domestic policies. I have seen his charismatic leadership capacity in action, in both Colombia and New York City. Through his many anecdotal and analytical reflections, I have learned a great deal about Colombia. Which is precisely why, from the very beginning of the writing process, Chucho has been directly involved in shaping the principal concepts enclosed in the book, refining a number of the initial ideas, adding further insight in some areas, and helping me think things through in a much more nuanced way in others. The book is written in the first person as a personal reflection, so I take full responsibility for the overall text, gaffes, style problems, and oversimplifications included. Nevertheless, it is fair to say that the broad view presented here reflects a vision that is more or less consistent with what I've understood to be the position of the popular social movements in Colombia. Chucho has been instrumental in helping me make this connection.

I would also like to thank Brendan Sweeney, a former student and now coconspirator whose meticulous research, unyielding skepticism, and excellent writing skills helped me considerably, particularly in filtering through much of the recent media coverage on Colombia, detailed in chapter 6.

Also valuable in this process were a number of people who took the time to read some of the initial sections of the book and made suggestions and comments: Included here are my colleague and friend Dr. Eduardo Duarte from Hofstra University, author Clara Nieto Ponce de León, and community activist Rafael Mutis. Adam Isacson of the Center for International Policy has also been an excellent resource for the latest information about Colombia and particularly U.S. policy debates. I should also thank everyone involved in the Colombia Media Project, whose forums, teach-ins, and conferences over the years have given me considerable direct access to some of the most courageous and brilliant minds that Colombia has to offer.

A special thanks goes to my friends and colleagues at WBAI and Pacifica Radio. Over the years the WBAI staff has been extremely supportive and indeed generous in opening up the limited resources of the station, allowing me to share the many voices struggling for justice in Colombia with the listeners of this important community media institution.

To Greg Ruggiero, my "paisano" and editor, I have considerable gratitude. His nonstop commitment to free speech and alternative forms of cultural and political expression has always been profoundly appreciated. His critical and meticulous editing style has also been a great support.

For all the familial warmth and loving hospitality that I've received upon every visit to this beautiful country, I want to thank the many members of the Maldonado and Murillo clans, especially Doña Barbarita, whose "tintos" and "almuerzos" not only made me feel right at home, but were essential in sustaining me as I put the finishing touches on the final draft.

And finally, a very warm, affectionate thank you to my beloved soul mate and *compañera*, Maria Victoria. Her thoughtful feedback on many of the ideas enclosed in these pages was immeasurable. And her strength, patience, and dedication have been an inspiration to me for many, many years, above and beyond the completion of this little book.

M.A.M.A.
Bogotá, Colombia—August 2003

Introduction

The date was September 19, 2001, and I was invited to present a lecture at a special screening of a feature documentary about the Colombian army's close links to right-wing death squads. The presentation was part of a month-long "international issues" series held annually at Hofstra University, and I had been assigned the task of placing the film into a broader historical context. Before arriving at the auditorium, I was a bit uncomfortable about the event itself, thinking that most of the audience would be focusing on the horrific events of the previous week and would have little interest in hearing about the war in Colombia. Organizers of the screening were also uncertain how the mixture of university students, faculty, and community guests would respond to the presentation, considering that the attacks on the Pentagon and the World Trade Center were so fresh on everybody's mind and made almost every other global development apparently irrelevant. But they insisted on seeing it through, precisely because of the urgency of the situation in Colombia. So I went with the hope that after watching the film we'd be able to discuss issues of terror and violence in a broader, indeed global context.

The film *Getting Away with Murder*, produced by Canadian independent filmmaker Daniel Bland, documents how the Colombian government's counterinsurgency strategy includes the use of paramilitary armies—described in some circles as "self-defense forces"—to displace civilian populations where left-wing guerrillas are said to operate, accusing anybody who has contact with the guerrillas as subversives, thus making them "legitimate" military targets. The process was implemented in other parts of the hemisphere and is based on the old U.S.-designed counterinsurgency philosophy of the need to "take the water away from the fish," the water being the civilian population and the fish being armed insurgents challenging the state, in this case rebels of the Revolutionary Armed Forces of Colombia, or FARC. According to journalists, former military officials, academics, and human rights workers interviewed in the film, this strategy was developed and executed in Colombia with a wink and a nod from the United States, which in the last decade has made Colombia the largest recipient of military assistance in the hemisphere, the third largest in the world, behind Israel and Egypt.[1] In the film, Bland graphically depicts the human costs of this policy, manifested most dramatically in the hundreds of civilian massacres carried out by the paramilitaries throughout the country, resulting in a massive wave of internal displacements that has swept Colombia since the early 1990s.

As the film's final credits were rolling up and the house lights were turned on, I began walking towards the podium with my notes in hand, for the first time in years a bit nervous about making a public presentation. No doubt the images in the film must have left an impression on the audience, but were they ready to hear more in light of events closer to home one week earlier? A number of students started filing out of the auditorium, I assumed to go to their next class. In that instance, I overheard one male student tell his friend with the enthusiasm of a baseball fan discussing the pennant race, "I think we should send these guys [meaning the Colombian army and its para-military allies] to Afghanistan to deal with the Taliban," one would guess to fight the war on terrorism. He added a slight chuckle at the end of his remark.

My initial trepidation about the day had been realized, and I was suddenly at a loss for words: People indeed were focusing on the terrorist attacks on the World Trade Center, and apparently nothing else in the world seemed to matter, regardless of its scope or magnitude. In the few seconds I had before my presentation, I tried to make sense of how the atrocious images of civilian massacres carried out by Colombia's parastate forces, in many cases with the indirect support of the United States, could be interpreted in this way. Slightly thrown off by his remarks, I began my talk by expressing disappointment in the way we can so easily glorify war abroad in the same breath that we condemn its effects in the rare occasion that it strikes us at home, as it did on September 11.

While this episode may appear on the surface to be minor and not worthy of citing in the introduction to a book about the conflict in Colombia, I believe it is relevant when considered within the context of the contemporary global climate, where terms such as terrorism, war, and security are being redefined to fit into the worldview that believes brutal force must be used to destroy any and all opposition, regardless of its origins or goals. The young man attending the screening, clearly unfamiliar with the nature of Colombia's internal war, was suggesting that the methods used by the paramilitaries should have been applied in Afghanistan, ostensibly to win "our" war against "terrorism."

That someone could justify the use of relentless violence, indeed state-sponsored terror against civilians, as a means to defend the national security interests of the United States, even if said with tongue in cheek, reflects the lethal combination of ignorance and arrogance that has defined U.S. international policy over the years. It is a line of thinking consistent with the U.S. National Security Strategy released by the Bush administration in September 2002, an official policy document that laid the foundations for the massive aerial bombardment and ground assault on Iraq and that even the *Washington Post* described as a shift from "deterrence to domination."[2] Complex situations are addressed with heavy-handed solutions, regardless of the long-term consequences. Unfortunately, this is a line of thinking embraced by many of Washington's closest allies around the world, including the government of Colombia.

It is safe to argue that there is widespread ignorance of the history of the internal conflict in Colombia and the roots of the current social, political, and economic crisis. This is coupled with a general lack of knowledge of the role Washington has played in this conflict. As a result, the situation in Colombia is easily framed by U.S. officials through the major information media as being completely chaotic, characterized by an international drug trade that has been fueling leftist guerrillas and right-wing paramilitaries in their war of terror against the Colombian state, itself almost defenseless, permanently under siege by these well-financed and heavily armed groups. This problem of drugs and violence in Colombia is destabilizing the entire region, the argument goes, and thus is a direct threat to the vital interests of the United States. As Representative Henry Hyde (R-IL) told Congress on March 6, 2002: "In our ongoing war against terrorism, we have an extremely volatile situation in our own hemisphere that cannot be ignored any longer: the threat against democracy in Colombia."[3] Otto Reich, the controversial, temporary undersecretary of state for interhemispheric affairs who was later unceremoniously removed from the post, put it simply in explaining that the United States must help Colombia by "training, arming, providing equipment and intelligence to the Colombian Armed Forces so that they could successfully execute their military strategy."[4]

The Colombian political establishment in turn plays its part in fomenting this narrow perspective, both domestically and on an international level, calling on Uncle Sam to be more active in helping defend "democracy" and restore "law and order," primarily through the fortification of the state's security apparatus. Again and again, different presidents have tried to make the case that things will get better only when the state defeats "the violent ones," meaning primarily the left-wing guerrilla groups that have been up in arms against the state since the early 1960s. Although some significant differences have existed over the years between the United States and Colombian governments, Colombian leaders come calling on Washington on a regular basis, saying all the right things relating to much needed economic reforms, Colombia's strong commitment to human rights, and its adoption of harder line antidrug policies, all in order to get what they need in terms of financial support and military hardware. Sovereignty is surrendered almost without question, allowing Washington to dictate everything from antidrug strategies and counterterrorism measures, to criminal justice, judicial reform, and extradition proceedings.

Whether it has been the decades-long war against "drug trafficking," the newly constituted war against "terrorism," or, as we have seen over the last few years, a convenient marriage of the two, the foundations of Colombia's internal conflict are rarely addressed by U.S. policymakers and are often swept under the rug by their Colombian counterparts. The pattern has continued with only slight variation over time: For the most part, the military approach toward the drug war in Colombia has remained at the forefront of the overall strategy. Fifteen years and billions of dollars later, the result has been very little progress in terms of actually curtailing the amount of drugs entering the United States, even by Washington's own stated objectives outlined in numerous studies and reports on drug trafficking. Colombia's history of institutionalized corruption, state neglect, far-reaching poverty, and political violence precedes by decades the introduction and expansion of the drug trade, a fact made irrelevant in a world driven by dramatic drug war images and succinct sound-bites by tough-talking politicians.

Ironically, over this period we have seen the rapid and widespread deterioration of the internal social-political conflict in Colombia. This is manifested in several areas, including the growth in right-wing paramilitary violence and an expansion of the left-wing armed insurgency, both resulting in a worsening human rights record that includes more than 2 million internal refugees. Meanwhile, notwithstanding claims of success made by both Colombian and U.S. officials in curtailing illicit crop cultivation as a result of accelerated aerial fumigations in Colombia, and leaving aside the potentially devastating health and environmental consequences the U.S.-backed coca eradication campaign may be having for the people living in the targeted areas—there has been an overall increase in production in other parts of the Andean region. Finally, as if to further demonstrate the overall failures of the ongoing policy, today more people are living in poverty in Colombia than in 1989, the result of an economic crisis unseen in the country since the 1930s.[5]

Fortunately for the hawks in Washington and Bogotá, today you have an added dimension in order to justify a continuation and expansion of the same failed policies: the war on "terrorism." For years, to varying degrees, Colombian and U.S. officials have attempted to link drug trafficking and the left-wing guerrilla organizations operating in Colombia, in particular the FARC. The term *narcoguerrilla* was coined in the mid-1980s by Lewis Tambs, the former U.S. ambassador to Colombia. He used it to describe how the FARC was using money extorted from coca farmers to fund its armed insurrection against the Colombian state. The term was quickly adopted by Colombian officials as they likened the guerrillas to another international drug cartel.

Gradually, the United States was forced to negate the legitimacy of the term as it became apparent that it was not exactly an accurate description of the FARC's relationship to the drug trade. Yes, the FARC taxed mid- and large-scale farmers, but its role in the drug trade at the time was really a drop in the bucket that paled in comparison to the billions of dollars being generated by those sectors involved in international trafficking, sectors in many instances tied directly to the state.

Nevertheless, with the dismantling of the notorious Medellín and Cali cocaine cartels in the early to mid-1990s, Colombian military officials began to adopt the term *narcoguerrilla* consistently, lobbying the U.S. Congress to loosen restrictions on counterdrug assistance in order to allow the armed forces to attack leftist rebels head-on with the latest military hardware. Their position was that they would be more effective fighting drugs if they could only get at the guerrillas, whom they accused of profiting immensely from the trade. But Congress, due to pressure from U.S.-based and Colombian human rights groups, resisted these requests for years, prohibiting military assistance designated for the drug war from being used against guerrillas in counterinsurgency operations for fear that it would lead to an explosion of human rights violations by the army. Furthermore, liberals kept raising the "Vietnam quagmire" in Washington, warning against a U.S. military entanglement in a situation that it could not so easily escape. These restrictions did not prevent the Colombian military from forging sinister links with outlawed paramilitary groups, from using intelligence to carry out hundreds of high-profile political assassinations, or from violating the human rights of noncombatants throughout the countryside. But at least the restrictions on U.S. aid allowed Washington to define its strategy as driven by counternarcotics objectives, not counterinsurgency, despite the fact that it maintained a primarily military focus.

Ironically, as peace talks between the FARC and the government of former President Andres Pastrana stumbled along in 1999 and 2000, U.S. counterdrug officials once again began to embrace the term *narcoguerrilla*, accusing the FARC of increasingly being directly involved in the drug trade, beyond the application of a "war tax" on coca growers, a process explained in more detail in chapter 3. Clinton drug czar Ret. General Barry McCaffrey said, "they've moved from being a terrorist group that only charged a tax on the production of the drug, to one that is actively involved as the dominant institution of production in the south of the country," while Randy Beers, head of the State Department's Office of Counter Narcotics Policy declared, "if the FARC are acting like drug traffickers, then we'll have to confront them as such, because the problem is ours as well." General Peter Pace, chief of the U.S. Southern Command at the time said, "it's clear for the world to see that within the drug trade there are members of FARC at every level," which was punctuated by Ana Maria Salazar, former undersecretary of defense, when she declared that this was "reflected in the kind of assistance we're providing to Colombia."[6] Therefore, despite Washington's public pledge of support to the fragile peace process between the rebels and the government, the case was being built *against* the FARC, making it more and more difficult for President Pastrana to seriously negotiate with the guerrilla high command. Today, as the current President Alvaro Uribe Vélez wages an all-out war against the guerrillas with the total support of the Bush administration, this seems like ancient history.

The Drug War on the Back Burner

Since September 11, 2001, the distinction between a counterinsurgency war and a war on drugs has become almost irrelevant as the United States expands its role in Colombia and the Colombian government implements its "Democratic

Defense and Security Policy." Almost immediately after the attacks on Washington and New York, the Bush White House successfully pushed forward a number of measures that allowed U.S. military aid to be used in offensive counterinsurgency missions in the name of the international war on terrorism, while expanding antidrug efforts that in recent years have been the source of great friction between the government and the rebels. The Bush administration also gutted former President Bill Clinton's 2000 directive limiting intelligence sharing with the Colombian armed forces to counter drug operations. United States operatives are now allowed to provide intelligence on guerrilla activity, making them active participants in the counterinsurgency war. Secretary of State Colin Powell made the argument quite simple when he said it was "necessary for us to give the government of Colombia assistance that is outside the counter-narcotics [activity] in order that they are able to deal with this threat to their survival as a nation."[7]

Today, both the Colombian and U.S. governments define the guerrillas as terrorists,[8] plain and simple. They are presented as a direct threat and enemy of the United States, recalling the heavy-handed rhetoric that President Ronald Reagan used to define the Sandinistas in Nicaragua in the 1980s. "Three hours by plane from Miami, we face a potential breeding ground for international terror equaled perhaps only by Afghanistan," said Representative Hyde. "The threat to the American interest is both imminent and clear."[9]

When the U.S. Justice Department indicted three members of the FARC on drug-trafficking charges in April 2002, Attorney General John Ashcroft described the rebel organization as "the most dangerous international terrorist group based in the Western Hemisphere," adding that the indictment marked the convergence of two U.S. priorities, serving as "a reminder that the lawlessness that breeds terrorism is also a fertile ground for the drug trafficking that supports terrorism."[10] For Ashcroft, it is lawlessness that breeds terrorism, fueled by narcodollars. That social dislocation, economic deprivation, and political and cultural marginalization might have something to do with it doesn't even cross his mind.

The State Department has kept the FARC and the other major rebel group, National Liberation Army (ELN), on its list of international terrorist organizations since 1997, so in a sense these kinds of statements were not new. What was new was the openness with which these groups were repeatedly being targeted by administration officials in the wake of September 11. Perhaps they were following the lead of the Colombian Right, which was also quick to link the attacks on the World Trade Center and the Pentagon with the violent actions carried out by the left-wing guerrillas throughout the country. In the weeks and months following September 11, it was not uncommon to see images of Osama Bin Laden and members of the Taliban edited into the news reports about FARC actions in Colombian television news broadcasts. Conservative politicians, church leaders, and members of the Colombian armed forces creatively developed new adjectives to describe Colombian rebels as "Talibanes" or "Bin Ladenes." This approach rendered any efforts at negotiating a political solution to the decades-long conflict as illegitimate, if not morally repugnant. It contributed to the demise of President Pastrana's futile efforts at peace, and to the election victory of right-wing President Uribe, who campaigned on a platform to defeat the guerrillas militarily as part of the war on terrorism.[11]

The end result was, once again, the endorsement of a primarily militaristic approach toward Colombia designed to confront a "terrorist threat" fueled by money from drug trafficking, a threat that is challenging not only a major democratic ally, but also the entire Andean region and, in turn, the United States itself. And once again, the other, primarily economic and political, motives behind this policy were rarely discussed. The complex social and political problems facing Colombia were reduced to nothing more than an extension of the global war on terrorism. The immediate and long-term impact that this military approach would have on the civilian population in Colombia became insignificant, primarily because the messages coming from both the Colombian and U.S. news media indicated that the people of Colombia supported a heavy-handed military solution. President Uribe's "landslide" election victory in May 2002 was described as a clear public endorsement for an expanded war because it was the first time in recent history that a second round was not needed to settle the presidential vote. The favorable opinion polls that followed Uribe throughout his first year in office provided the icing on the cake.

Upon taking office on August 7, 2002, amid a wave of violent attacks on the presidential palace attributed to the guerrillas that resulted in twenty-one deaths, Uribe declared an all-out war against guerrillas, committing himself to defeating them militarily through a series of controversial measures. He imposed a state of internal commotion that automatically curtailed a number of civil protections. Despite a substantial fiscal deficit, Uribe expanded the defense budget to be paid for by a new war tax on the Colombian people. He established special "rehabilitation and consolidation zones" in the most contested regions of the country, giving extraordinary powers to military authorities. And he promoted restrictive antiterrorism legislation within the Colombian Congress that human rights groups described as a reversal of the gains made during the 1991 process of constitutional reform. In stark contrast with his predecessor Andres Pastrana, who pledged to carry out a peace dialogue with the guerrillas to end the decades-long internal conflict, Uribe vowed to win the war against these "terrorists" through military force. In Uribe's eyes, Colombia does not have an internal political-military conflict, but a law and order problem. The guerrillas are not an armed opposition force, but armed bandits involved in unrepentant terror. It was a vision consistent with the way the White House viewed the world after September 11. U.S. military aid, for years limited to fighting the "war on drugs," was now being made available to fight a counterinsurgency war, something human rights groups in both countries had been concerned about for years. Whereas the counterdrug motives behind U.S. policy had become increasingly suspect, who could argue against a policy designed to counter terrorism in the wake of recent global events? President Bush's "war on terrorism" had successfully established its Andean front. Opposition to these positions went unreported.

Two Views on Terrorism

In the immediate aftermath of the World Trade Center attacks, I was heartened by the communications I began to receive from friends living in Colombia, many of whom shared a number of interesting concerns relating to state-sponsored terror, collective violence, victimization, and justice. One of the first messages I received was an e-mail from a young indigenous friend living in southwest Colombia. A Páez Indian from the department of Cauca who is involved in a popular media-and-education project for indigenous youth, he first expressed concern about how my family and I were faring in the wake of the collapse of the World Trade Center towers, having seen the cinema-like images repeatedly on television. He then described in poetic detail how the pain of the families who were victimized by the attacks was shared by his people, themselves victims for years of terror, albeit of a different kind.

Then he suddenly shifted his focus and began to interpret what the tragic events may mean in the short and long term for the United States. Echoing what others have expressed since September 11, he pointed out that the terror attack for the first time put the U.S. public in direct contact with fear *en carne propria*—in the flesh—something known before only in the movies. He reminded me that his community has lived with this kind of fear for generations, and as a result he sympathized deeply with us up "in the north." With considerable optimism and a degree of naïveté, he said that perhaps this traumatic experience would have a long-term positive impact on the U.S. public by bringing the people "closer to understanding the rest of the world," and make the people finally understand the "millions of us who have been forced to live in a constant fear," very often due to policies developed in the United States.

In the weeks after the terrorist attacks, I thought closely about what my friend in Cauca meant by these words, and repeated them regularly whenever I spoke to others about the "war on terrorism," the tragedy of September 11, and Colombia itself. I then found myself constantly comparing what he said with the profoundly different perspective expressed by the young man I described earlier who exited the film screening with his off-the-cuff remark about how to deal with the Taliban. Two years removed from those events, it has become alarmingly apparent that these distinct views have been moving on a dangerous collision course, with the latter unfortunately dominating the world arena and the major centers of power, to the detriment of the millions of people around the world who were hoping for the former to take hold. In Iraq, we saw it reduced to a type of football game, presented through the lens of embedded reporters and high-tech digital graphics. It happened so quickly that one would think that the long-term effects of such an enterprise are nonexistent. In Colombia, we can clearly see the effects of this clash of perceptions, but it appears that nobody is paying attention. It may take years before the tides begin to shift.

In the following pages, I will try to make sense of the conflict in Colombia by rejecting wholeheartedly the frame in which the Bush administration has placed it, that is, within his vision about global "terrorism." Many scholars, analysts, and activists have argued that the drug war was a way for the United States to maintain its military and economic domination of the Western Hemisphere in the wake of the Cold War. The war on terrorism allows this to continue, but perhaps with more possibilities for public relations that would justify the relentless application of U.S. military power.

There is no question that to a large extent Bush's vision is being imposed around the world without the existence of a universal consensus, as we saw, for example, in early 2003 when Germany, France, Russia, and China remained steadfast in their resistance to Washington's belligerent stance on Iraq. In this hemisphere, Mexico, Chile, and Brazil have demonstrated a reluctance to embrace Bush's militarist policies wholeheartedly, not to mention the expected troublemakers in Cuba and Venezuela. However, it must be pointed out that the vision promoted by President Bush *is* shared by most of Colombia's political establishment, which, although by no means homogeneous, does believe it to be in Colombia's interest to maintain good relations with the world's only superpower. As polls seem to indicate, a good percentage of the Colombian people are also in accordance, apparently embracing the get-tough stance of President Uribe.[12]

In part, this is understandable. Security and terrorism have been real concerns in Colombia for decades, not only for the ruling elite, but also for a broad cross section of the population. The senseless terrorist bombing of an exclusive Bogotá social club in February 2003 that killed thirty-six people and wounded 160 struck a chord within Colombia's elite, horrified by the carnage that occurred in a central point of their everyday social encounters. Less than a week later, the detonation of explosives in a house in the southern town of Neiva killed another fifteen, this time mostly poor residents of the community, the usual victims of the violence in Colombia. Clearly, there are calls for an end to business as usual coming from many directions and distinct sectors. The vast majority of the Colombian people are tired of war, of politically motivated violence, of terror. The fundamental problem is that the loudest voices, or at least those given the greatest echo in the primary information media of both countries, are calling for more of the same in the name of change. Force becomes the primary solution, jettisoning any and all constructive alternatives.

A false consensus has emerged that embraces military solutions to the problem, manifested most clearly in President Uribe, a powerful figure who has commanded the respect of the Colombian people because of his direct language, his intense work ethic, and his commitment to efficiency as a way to weed out government corruption. There is no question that his frank public style is refreshing in a country with a long history of leaders who spoke from both sides of their mouths. But what stands out most is his uncompromising disdain for the guerrillas, the perpetrators of the kidnapping and murder of his own father. This in a sense has provided him the moral justification for the "mano dura" approach he has taken. The "drug war" is now a war against "terror." There will be no compromise with terrorists. But will the hard-line approach solve Colombia's profound social, economic, and political problems? This is a question I'll attempt to answer within the pages of this book.

In the following chapters, I will examine how the conflict in Colombia is not about drugs, nor guerrillas, nor "terrorism," but rather about the unwillingness of the country's elite to open up spaces for truly democratic participation in areas of economic and social development and political representation. The state's refusal to be responsive to the public good lies at the root of the civil war. The extreme polarization of Colombian society is the direct result. The drug trade is undoubtedly a significant problem that in many substantial ways has exacerbated the situation and penetrates just about every sector of Colombian society. But remove it from the equation and keep everything else in place as is, and you will still have profound civil conflict.

The book is divided into three parts. In Part I, I focus on the origins of the conflict in order to place the current juncture into a historic context. In chapter 1, I begin by describing some of the major myths surrounding Colombian democracy, which for generations have been embraced by the country's elite to maintain its domination of political and economic power. I argue that the perpetuation of these myths—political, economic, and cultural—allows both Colombian and U.S. officials to formulate policies that have repeatedly failed and in many ways have made matters worse. In chapter 2, I examine the historical evolution of the decades-long civil war, going back about sixty years in Colombia's history, as opposed to starting way back in the colonial period and Colombia's early independence. Although this earlier period should by no means be forgotten and is in many respects still present with us today, it is safe to say that the current phase of Colombia's tumultuous history began more or less during the post-World War II era.

In Part II, I introduce the reader in greater detail to the principal actors involved in today's conflict. In chapter 3, I provide an overview of Colombia's guerrilla movements, with a particular focus on the evolution and growth of the FARC and the role it currently plays in the civil war. Today the guerrillas are presented as the primary obstacles to peace and are criticized almost daily for carrying out acts of terror. To a certain extent this may be correct. Nonetheless, I will show how the guerrillas have provided the justification for state-sponsored terrorism in Colombia, manifested most clearly in the emergence of the right-wing paramilitary groups mentioned at the outset who, for the most part, have targeted civilians generally and the popular movement specifically as part of the state's larger counterinsurgency strategy. As we will see in chapter 4, the implementation of this paramilitary strategy is directly reflective of the main myths about Colombian society outlined earlier. By looking at the "demobilization" process launched in 2003 between the Uribe government and the leadership of the paramilitary organizations, I will show how impunity once again seems to be ruling the day, a dangerous development for the future of the country. Here, where applicable, I will demonstrate how the United States has been complicit in this state-sponsored terror and why very little, if anything, has been done to change the situation, making today's "war on terror" in the Colombian context outright hypocrisy.

Part III focuses on U.S. policy and perceptions. In chapter 5, I will describe the way in which U.S. policy toward Colombia has evolved prior to and since September 11, elaborating on some of the points mentioned in this Introduction. Here we will see most clearly how the long history of conflict in Colombia is almost religiously ignored in Washington, with the complicity of Colombia's political and military leadership who are so dependent on U.S. assistance. Because one would think that in a democracy like the United States the news media would be among the first to point out the contradictions in government policy, chapter 6 will feature a brief examination of the U.S. media's coverage of the conflict. Here we'll see how, very often, they too are complicit in the hypocrisy.

Finally, in conclusion, in chapter 7 I will briefly point to some alternatives to the current mode of thinking, with a general introduction to some of the popular voices of Colombia's social movements that, amid a climate of rampant political violence and repression, have been mobilizing for years against state neglect, government corruption, and the dark forces of terror. Therefore, I will try to show how, notwithstanding the constant attacks against them from all sides in the conflict, their collective struggle for a new Colombia has been growing in force in recent years, challenging both the intransigence of the Colombian state and the interventionism of the United States. In my view, these groups provide the best hope for the future of a truly democratic Colombia, which is precisely why they pose the greatest threat to the status quo arrangement built by policymakers in Washington and Bogotá.

I

Origins of the Conflict

1

The Myths Behind Colombian Democracy

The nature of Colombia's internal conflict has been completely distorted by the prism of drug-war politics. This has resulted in fundamentally inaccurate views about Colombian society that permeate U.S. policymaking circles, the news and information media, and public opinion as a whole. There is a general tendency to look at Colombia as a violent, drug-producing country that is living through an extended period of uncontrollable crisis and chaos, characterized by random murders, massacres, and other acts of senseless bloodshed committed by ruthless criminals. As seen from the United States, this violence is a direct threat to Colombia's democratic institutions and can be remedied only with extreme measures. The people trying to defend Colombia's democracy, under constant attack from undemocratic forces, must be supported in the interest of the United States and the region as a whole.

Ironically, although this negative image has angered Colombians for years, it is very often used by the Colombian political and economic elite to promote its own agenda abroad: "We need the support of the international community in weeding out these violent ones; after all, our democracy is at stake." A variation of this oversimplification of the problem has been repeated countless times by different governments, the end result being that the violence is presented in a vacuum, completely detached from its root causes. In this way, Colombian officials are able to muffle criticism of the undemocratic political system, the gross economic inequalities, and the far-reaching levels of social and cultural marginalization facing the vast majority of the people. Indeed, while being concerned about the erroneous public perceptions foreigners may have about Colombia, they simultaneously embrace them, all the while failing to address the causes of the country's deep problems, which lie in a political culture of profound intolerance and repression.

As it turns out, Colombians and U.S. citizens are often equally guilty of harboring faulty perceptions about the internal conflict in Colombia and, perhaps more significantly, its origins and potential solutions. I've been able to witness it from both perspectives as a Colombian-American with deep ties to both the United States and Colombia. Many of us in the North see Colombia the way we see it because of the arrogance and ethnocentrism that comes from living in the most powerful country in the world. We have to put things in order for "those people" down South. Colombians, on the other hand, reflect a vision of righteous indignation that comes from years of "victimhood," in terms both of living through a real war that has affected millions of lives in a direct and personal way, and of suffering from the stereotypes that have emerged as a result of that war. In both cases, there is a dangerous tendency to stick our collective heads in the sand.

There is no question that Colombia is a complex country, making it difficult for people to try to make sense of it. But it is not too complicated to understand if one takes the time to study the roots of the contemporary conflict, the diverse actors involved therein, and the role that the United States has played on many levels, politically, economically, and militarily. Unfortunately, on the one hand you have a U.S. public spoon-fed an erroneous picture of Colombia as a drug and security concern, and on the other you have a small but growing sector of Colombian society that is convinced that if you wipe out the guerrillas, "los violentos," you'll solve all of the country's problems. Both visions are grounded in a series of myths directly tied to the deep-rooted contradictions that shape contemporary Colombian history. Before going into the details of that history, I find it necessary to briefly outline these myths.

Colombian officials often boast about having the "longest standing democracy in Latin America," but throughout its recent history the spoils of that democracy have gone to a very small, privileged sector of society, what journalist and writer Apolinar Díaz Callejo described as "hereditary power without monarchy."[1] In Colombia, the Constitution and its laws are often ignored and rarely enforced, either because of a lack of bureaucratic capacity on the part of the state to do so, or because of an absence of political will on the part of the ruling elite to execute those laws that are designed to protect the public.

The statistic that most dramatically illustrates this is that of all the political crimes committed in Colombia every year—including assassinations, forced disappearances, extrajudicial executions, and torture—97 percent end up in complete impunity.[2] On average, anywhere between 2,100 and 3,000 people are killed each year for political reasons in Colombia.[3] This occurs despite the fact that, during the past sixty years, Colombia has been ruled only once by a military dictatorship, from 1953 to 1957. The country avoided the "national security dictatorships" that emerged in the southern cone of South America in the 1960s, 1970s, and 1980s. Colombia has presidential elections every four years, as well as elections for other national, departmental, and local offices where political parties openly compete for votes using the communications media as their primary vehicle for democratic discourse. It has witnessed dozens of "peaceful" transitions of political power on every occasion since 1957, something not every country in the region could easily claim. Today, talk of political reform is openly debated in the news media, all in an effort to strengthen Colombian "democracy."

Since its independence in 1810, and certainly over the last sixty years, political life in Colombia has been dominated by two powerful, traditional parties, Conservative and Liberal, while the army, despite tensions over the years with the civilian leadership, has remained subordinate to the elite political establishment.[4] Conservatives have always been identified with large landowners and the rigid hierarchy of the Catholic Church, while Liberals have often been characterized as more reform-minded, although with strong links to powerful economic interests as well. As historian David Bushnell writes, "constitutional government in Colombia has endured at least partly because it has suited the interests of the wealthy and powerful."[5]

Nevertheless, the open elections, U.S.-styled campaigns, and regular parliamentary debates that characterize Colombian bourgeois politics have provided the Colombian elite with a convenient argument that democracy can indeed work in Colombia, if only it were given more support from outside. These existing democratic formalities have provided the Colombian establishment with a smokescreen from which it can point to the violent, antidemocratic, guerrilla forces and paramilitaries as the greatest threat to its democratic institutions, while very rarely having to look itself in the mirror and be held accountable for the many undemocratic practices that have been carried out against popular sectors for the last fifty years.

Political Violence and "Democracy"

The fact of the matter is that the level of politically motivated violence generated by the state and its paramilitary apparatus, ostensibly in response to increasingly high levels of guerrilla-generated violence, has in many respects surpassed the brutality witnessed anywhere else in the region. Notwithstanding the existence of at least the superficial trappings of a democratic political culture, what exists in Colombia are two parallel spheres that negate the existence of a genuine democracy, as Father Javier Giraldo of the Colombian human rights group Justicia y Páz wrote in 1996. The first is the bureaucratic/administrative sphere, where traditional political parties, run predominantly by elites, compete for the spoils that "serve as an incentive for cycles of generalized corruption," all the while neglecting the needs of the majority of the people. The second is the country's social conflict, whose origins lie in the collective attempts at resistance to the first sphere, and which over the years has been turned over to the armed forces and its auxiliaries for management, with dramatic levels of repression.[6]

This repression is part of Colombia's long history, although one would be hard pressed to find even a mention of it in any of the hundreds of contemporary news reports about the conflict, in either the U.S. or the Colombian media. Indeed, the failure of Colombia's "democratic" institutions to respond to the public's legitimate, constitutionally protected demands regarding the right to life, employment, land, political participation, economic opportunity, and justice, and the tendency of the state to respond to these demands through the use of force, has led some sectors of Colombian society to take up arms to achieve their political and social objectives. It is a complex picture that can be summed up with several general observations, the first of which has already been made: Colombia on paper is a liberal democracy, but in reality it is far from satisfying a democracy's basic prerequisites, precisely because, as Colombian sociologist and journalist Alfredo Molano has pointed out, the power monopoly of the two traditional parties, "which have an aura almost of religious trappings," has prevented social changes "unleashed by development from finding suitable avenues of political action."[7]

Second, although economically Colombia is a rich country with considerable natural resources and productive capacity, not everyone has benefited from this wealth. In its ongoing effort to stimulate foreign investment, Colombian officials often point out that until its most recent economic recession, the country has avoided the major crises other countries of the region faced in the 1980s and 1990s.[8] Notwithstanding the relative stability and wealth of the country, one cannot erase the fact that the majority of Colombians are poor, with between 60 and 68 percent of the population currently living at or below the poverty line. One might expect this in the countryside where the economic situation is much worse, with poverty levels reaching 85 percent. However, poverty is universal in Colombia. For example, in the Caribbean city of Cartagena, perhaps the most popular tourist attraction in all of Colombia, almost half of the population lives in absolute misery, while 75 percent (more than 700,000 people) are forced to survive below the poverty level. These numbers are not so readily apparent to the millions of annual visitors to the city's sandy beaches and walled-in historic sector.[9] Next to Brazil, Colombia has the most inequitable distribution of wealth in the Western Hemisphere.

To understand the social impact these economic statistics ultimately have on working people, consider the experience of one displaced peasant farmer I interviewed in August 2001. He was one of about 150 people living in makeshift wooden shacks built alongside a sewage waste dump on the outskirts of San Jose, the capital of the southern department of Guaviare in the northernmost stretch of Colombia's Amazon region. He had recently lost his small farm in the Guaviare countryside, a victim of the forced displacement that has terrorized Colombia in recent years. His two sons left home about a year earlier to find employment because there was absolutely no work for them in San Jose. As it turns out, his older son joined the FARC rebels, while the younger one joined the paramilitaries. Under such conditions, one cannot honestly talk about the existence of a democracy. Problems of this nature do not require military solutions.

Together with the political and economic myths that have sustained Colombian democracy, there is a third myth relating to the concept of the Colombian nation. Colombian leaders have always embraced and promoted the false notion of Colombia as a unified republic with a population sharing the same socio-cultural values of the ruling, primarily European elite. Certainly the existence of Colombian nation*ness* cannot be negated, exemplified by the universal excitement when the national *fútbol* team performs well, when one of its musical artists is recognized on an international stage like the Grammys, or when its former president is named the general secretary of the Organization of American States. Novelist Gabriel García Márquez's winning the Nobel Prize in literature was widely seen as a celebration of Colombian literary achievement. Whether or not they like her music, Colombians across the board applaud the crossover success of pop sensation Shakira. Colombians watched Major League Baseball's All-Star Game in 2003 not because they're big baseball fans but because they wanted to see Edgar Renteria in action.

But Colombian nation*hood* is superficial at best, and its history since independence is a reflection of a failure of the nation-state to establish principles of social protections that blanket the public, regardless of class, regional, and, perhaps most significantly, racial origin. The profound regionalism that exists is difficult to comprehend, although when traveling around the country it strikes you immediately. Fishermen living along the Caribbean coast have absolutely no connection to the indigenous farmers of the Amazonian region, while middle-class Bogotanos find little commonality with Afro-Colombian peasants in the banana-growing region of the Pacific coast. These are just a few of the many regionalisms that exist, ignored daily in the halls of power. As one Independent member of Congress told me recently, "people in the city could care less about what happens to the campesino in the countryside. It's as if they live in two different countries."

It becomes more problematic when one considers the issue of race and Colombia's extraordinary cultural diversity. The myth of a "racial democracy" in Colombia is pervasive. The fact that the country is and always has been divided strongly along ethnic and racial lines—with those wielding power consistently of European descent based in the capital and other major central urban centers, and the most marginalized sectors being either indigenous, of African descent, or a combination of the races—is repeatedly ignored or simply given lip service by the same institutions established to defend the country's democratic traditions.[10] This issue is very rarely raised when contemporary Colombian politics are discussed, even within progressive circles inside Colombia. It also doesn't occur to the people shaping U.S. policy.

The fact of the matter is that Colombia is a multicultural, pluriethnic country where discrimination and marginalization of black and indigenous people have been institutionalized. This can be seen in the fact that of the more than 2 million Colombians who have been internally displaced as a result of the civil war over the past ten years, more than one-third are of African descent. Colombia has a large black population, ranging anywhere between 20 and 45 percent of the total, depending on which figures you read and how you interpret them.[11] Eighty percent of Afro-Colombians live with their basic needs unmet in conditions of poverty, with an annual per capita income of 600 U.S. dollars (the national average is $1,500); some 74 percent of all Afro-Colombians receive salaries below the legal minimum wage; in the Pacific coast, where 85 percent of the population is of African descent, only 43 percent of all homes in urban areas have running water served by an aqueduct, while the number drops to 5 percent in rural areas. Illiteracy rates in Colombia's black population range between 20 percent in urban areas and 45 percent in rural areas, double the national average.[12] In short, Afro-Colombians have been subjected to a history of institutionalized violence, intense racial discrimination, a lack of opportunity to participate in the economic life of the country, and the complete disrespect of their culture.

For the indigenous communities of Colombia, the situation is not much better. There are eighty-four different indigenous groups in Colombia, of which sixty-five have maintained their own language. Making up less than 5 percent of the overall population (there are about 2 million in total), Colombia's indigenous people continue to be threatened almost daily by the violence of the internal conflict, as all the armed actors attempt to gain the strategic upper hand in their territories. In fact, there is a growing amount of evidence demonstrating the deliberate displacement of Afro-Colombian and indigenous communities because they happen to populate large areas deemed strategically and economically important for the "national well-being." All of these points are worth mentioning as we try to understand the nature of Colombia's "democracy." Colombia's political leadership seldom talks about the extreme marginalization of indigenous and Afro-Colombian communities and the role the state has played in maintaining the racist status quo when they appeal to international public opinion about the threats its brand of democracy faces from so-called terrorist groups.

Colombia's Media Institutions: Part of the Problem

Behind this backdrop we find the Colombian mass communication system. Colombia's media institutions have been described as an "imperfect duopoly" where two major groups control the majority of the information industries.[13] They continue to perpetuate the above-mentioned myths about Colombian society, by embracing the institutional definitions used by the establishment to describe the fringes of society, or by limiting the spaces whereby these voices may be heard.[14] As in other parts of the world, Colombian media scholars have pointed out repeatedly that when it comes to journalism and democracy, "political and economic interests are more important than support for freedom of expression and the right of citizens to information."[15] Yet again and again, the existence of a "free press" is used by Colombian officials as still another example of the strength of Colombian democracy.

Therefore, from the notions of a liberal democracy severely tainted by political violence and repression, of relative economic stability built alongside abject misery, of "racial and national unity" based on European supremacy, we see an institutional process of exclusion, much of which has been downplayed, if not outright ignored, by the dominant domestic media industries and, as we will see later, their counterparts abroad.

It is in response to these fundamental contradictions inherent in Colombian "democracy" that many varied popular movements have emerged over the years, in essence with the goal of forcing the state to be responsive to the majority of the people. In most cases, these groups have carried out their struggle in the form of legal resistance, whether manifested as peasant and indigenous organizing over land reform, "civic strikes" of the popular movement, trade unions mobilizing over workers' rights, or political independents engaged in grassroots, sometimes populist, strategies to broaden the political spaces monopolized by elites. Yet their efforts have been met by direct and indirect repression, resulting in tens of thousands of deaths, arbitrary detentions, cases of torture, and forced disappearances or exile.

This has led others to resort to armed solutions, as exemplified by the many guerrilla groups that have formed over the last forty years. The most visible today is the Revolutionary Armed Forces of Colombia (FARC), currently considered the oldest and largest leftist insurgency in all of the Americas.

The history of contemporary Colombia, therefore, is about the varying degrees to which the Colombian state has perpetuated the myths outlined in this chapter while refusing to address the root causes of the intense social and political conflict that has existed for decades. The dramatic escalation of the conflict, exemplified by the evolution of the guerrillas and the government's responses to them—issues I will address in-depth in the following chapters—should be understood within this context.

2

Colombia's Un-Civil Conflict:
A History That Repeats Itself

In order to understand the complex nature of Colombia's internal conflict and the many actors involved, we must reject out of hand the simplistic argument that today's left-wing guerrilla armies are the cause of all of the country's ills. As we'll see in this chapter, throughout the history of Colombia's contemporary civil war, nobody has held the exclusive franchise on political violence and the use of terror against civilians. Indeed, Colombia's history since its independence in 1810 has been characterized in this way. As Colombian author Arturo Alape wrote in one of his most important books, *La paz, la violencia*:

> Testigos de excepción: "Since the beginning it was clear that the State wasn't for everybody, and its control by a few needed to be maintained, lost or won by employing the only methods known until then by the leadership class that emerged from the war of independence: using war itself.[1]

The "structural elements of violence, the inherited hatreds, the partisan passions, the displacement from lands, the religious persecutions, the political partition of the country and the physical elimination of one's political adversary" shaped

Colombian history throughout the nineteenth century. It continued unchanged into the twentieth and was revamped "with even more force" by the 1940s.[2] It is this latter period that will serve as my starting point in attempting to understand today's internal crisis.

La Violencia and the National Front

The emergence of the Revolutionary Armed Forces of Colombia (FARC) and the National Liberation Army (ELN) in the early 1960s, and their expansion in the 1980s and 1990s, is directly related to the lack of political spaces that characterize Colombian political history, especially since the formation of the National Front in 1958, the power-sharing arrangement set up by the Liberals and Conservatives in the wake of Colombia's only recent flirtation with military dictatorship. This will be explained in greater detail below.

Today's guerrillas can trace their roots back to the peasant struggles of the 1920s and 1930s, but more recently to one of the bloodiest periods in contemporary Colombian history known as *La Violencia*, the Violence. *La Violencia* took place in a post–World War II climate in Colombia where three-quarters of the population was made up of peasants, more than half the people were illiterate, and more than 50 percent of the land was controlled by less than 3 percent of the landowners.[3] At the time, a series of laws and security measures were being enacted that were designed to protect the landowning aristocracy against potential incursions and takeovers by an increasingly impatient peasantry, for years denied any true access to productive land. So, as was the case in other parts of the world, the conflict in Colombia arose over the struggle for land. However, *La Violencia* was much more than a simple turf battle between the two major parties and their differing views about land reform.

Although *La Violencia* pitted armed groups supportive of Liberal Party reformists against the Conservative oligarchy resistant to land-reform measures that would have eliminated ancestral privilege to land titles, it was not simply a case of "interparty warfare," as the Colombian establishment today often erroneously describes it. Indeed, *La Violencia* was initiated by the Conservative government of Mariano Ospina Perez, who won the presidency in 1946 when a split within the Liberal Party prevented it from prevailing in the election, despite being the majority party. Ospina and the Conservative leadership, with the support of the Catholic Church hierarchy and the military, launched a campaign of brutal repression against the Liberal bases, particularly in the countryside. A process of demonization was unleashed that targeted the Liberal Party in the state-controlled media, in the pulpit, and in the halls of Congress—eventually suspended by President Ospina. Tens of thousands of peasants tied to the Liberal Party were killed. The armed groups that emerged were therefore resisting the deliberate state-sponsored violence.

It was within this environment of intense repression and conflict that the charismatic leader Jorge Eliécer Gaitán emerged. He created a movement based on the reformist themes of economic redistribution, political participation, and a rejection of the dual-party domination of power, themes that continue to fuel the demands of the popular social movements. These ideas generated widespread support in the mid-1940s, especially within the working classes of Colombia's major urban centers. In a country historically torn by partisan strife between Liberals and Conservatives, Gaitán was able to achieve something quite uncommon. As Colombian historian Gonzalo Sánchez writes in a thoughtful, comprehensive historical essay about the period, by the mid-1940s Gaitán "had succeeded in creating a new historical force made up of the popular classes united across traditional party lines."[4] Although Gaitán was a member of the Liberal Party and eventually assumed its leadership, his slogans and speeches against the dual-party oligarchy actually set him apart from the traditional power structures of Colombia. He represented in many ways a truly revolutionary break from Colombia's closed political past and was seen as a direct threat by many of the country's most powerful political leaders, Liberal and Conservative alike.

Gaitán's assassination on April 9, 1948—as Colombia was preparing to host the ninth Pan-American Congress—triggered weeks of spontaneous popular protests, looting, and riots in the streets of Bogotá. To this day, Gaitán's murder has not been fully resolved, the intellectual authors have never been brought to justice, and the case remains a symbol of the extreme levels of impunity that have always existed in Colombia. Most accounts point to the Conservatives as the culprits, given the level of violence that the Party's militants were already responsible for throughout the country. Some analysts said disgruntled Liberals may have been behind the murder, although this theory is not as likely. Still others point to the growing concern from Washington over Gaitán's rapid rise within Colombian national politics as a possible reason for his untimely demise. The U.S. government's preoccupation with Gaitán was reflected in the frequent dispatches to Washington by John C. Wiley, U.S. Ambassador to Colombia in 1946–1947, who described the charismatic leader as a person who "would try to deplume our eagle and lift in flight the wings of charlatanism," a "demagogue who "blindly promoted state socialism" and that "will be an important political concern for some time."[5]

Regardless of who was behind the murder, the result was a massive spontaneous response on the part of Gaitán's supporters, who hit the streets in a rage now referred to in Colombian history books as *El Bogotazo*. What this uprising was unable to do, however, was establish the mechanism to systematically and effectively, through an organized, indeed revolutionary process, confront the oligarchic rule that had led to the popularity of Gaitanísmo in the first place. In the wake of Gaitán's assassination, measures were implemented to eliminate what Sánchez describes as "the possibility that the worker's movement might become the articulator of social protest and political opposition," including the firing of militant workers, the purging of the most independent union leaders, the criminalization of strikes as a means of legitimate social protest, and the destruction of a united union movement.[6] The democratic spaces that Gaitán was trying to open up were immediately closed in the aftermath of his murder. To many, Gaitán's assassination serves as the symbol of democracy aborted, an act that has been repeated over and over with the murders of hundreds of charismatic leaders on a local, regional, and national level throughout the country.

The Liberal Party, meanwhile, eager to play a role in the reestablishment of order and concerned about losing its cherished space in the elite two-party power structure, distanced itself from the masses of protesters who emerged in the streets after their leader was gunned down. For the most part, Liberal Party officials acquiesced and participated in the clampdown on the popular protesters. Nevertheless, in the eyes of Conservatives, these efforts were seen as cosmetic at best, opportunistic at worst. Certainly the Liberal role in the clampdown was not enough, and Liberals of all stripes once again became the targets of the sweeping political assassinations, massacres, and direct physical threats that had been launched under the Ospina government even before Gaitán's assassination. The armed resistance by bands of peasants loyal to the Liberal Party continued, as Colombian society polarized even further.[7]

What followed was years of relentless violence throughout the country, characterized by a general state of terror and profound partisan sectarianism. The violence pitted community against community, neighbor against neighbor, and led to some of the most ruthless episodes in Colombia's bloody history. As Gonzalo Sánchez writes, "an entire generation was growing up whose attitudes towards their condition oscillated between fatalism, a thirst for vengeance, and repressed rebellion."[8]

The mantle of violence and repression was passed from Ospina to the ultra-Conservative, neofascist politician Laureáno Gómez, who assumed the presidency in 1950 after elections where the Liberal Party did not participate. Gómez was committed to maintaining Colombia's erupting social divisions comfortably within the dimensions of Liberal versus Conservative battles. Now that Gaitán had been silenced, the entire Liberal party had to be made illegitimate in the eyes of the Colombian people. It should be pointed out that the government of Laureáno Gómez gained considerable mileage from the anticommunist climate that was emerging in Washington after World War II. His ruthless approach to dealing with the peasant guerrillas was presented as evidence to the United States that, like Batista in Havana, Somoza in Managua, and Trujillo in Santo Domingo, Washington had a good friend in the presidential palace in Bogotá. While these other countries could be described as long-term hegemonic dictatorships that were a far cry from the political evolution that led to Gómez's rise to power in Colombia, all of them used ruthless repression of internal opposition to carry out policies favorable to U.S. interests. It should be pointed out that Gómez was the only Latin American leader who supported the U.S. war effort in Korea by actually sending Colombian forces to the region. The stability of his government was seen as consistent with Washington's long-term interests. Despite the different historical juncture in which we find ourselves in the early years of the twenty-first century, the general position of the United States back then was remarkably similar to what we see today. In Washington's eyes, the Colombian government was fighting for its survival against armed bandits in guerrilla enclaves that represented a challenge to the pre-existing (undemocratic) social order, regardless of whether they were communist-inspired or not. Today of course conditions are quite different, but there are similarities: the bandits are now called "terrorists."

The violence continued, as did the resistance to Gómez. It led to massive levels of displacement and sweeping land colonization in areas of southern Tolima, in the middle Magdalena Valley, in parts of Cauca and the Cauca Valley, and in the eastern plains or "llanos." A highly fragmented guerrilla movement was emerging with complex political and social roots, depending on the area where they were principally operating. The guerrilla enclaves gradually evolved into areas of refuge for peasants fleeing the violence and centers of resistance to government authority. Initially these armed groups maintained links with the Liberal directorate, looking at the urban-based, elite leadership of the party to lead the charge of revolt against the Conservative government of Gómez. But as the stakes were raised and resistance to the government-led violence escalated, the Liberal establishment once again abandoned its connections with the popular resistance, in this case the guerrillas. Connected to these groups were armed groups linked to the Communist Party, who in some areas forged alliances with Liberals in their battles against Conservatives. The armed groups developed a strategy of resistance that in many respects was revolutionary, combining a military component with intense political mobilizing within the civilian population.[9]

This process of extreme violence and organized resistance continued for several years, affecting every aspect of the country's development. It culminated in a military coup that led to removal of the Conservative Gómez and the installation of the dictatorship of General Gustavo Rojas Pinilla in June 1953. General Rojas Pinilla was an anticommunist strongman who, like Gómez, had ties to Washington, but, unlike Gómez, was seen with favorable eyes by members of both parties, who looked to him as the solution to the escalating violence. He was greeted enthusiastically by all sides in the conflict, in particular the Liberals. General Rojas Pinilla carried out a series of military amnesties for the armed guerrillas, promoting a vision of national unity as opposed to the partisan sectarianism that was destroying the country.

For the most part, the armed groups agreed as the government began formulating a program of democratic reform and economic development that was ostensibly designed to reconstruct a devastated countryside and assist its displaced peasantry. The vast, underdeveloped regions of the south were opened up as solutions to the land problem, leading to intense colonization by peasants displaced by the violence. Some armed guerrilla groups, particularly those based in the communist-influenced area of Sumapáz and southern Tolima, were not quite ready to take part in the amnesty, however, and opted for more of a "self-defense" approach to the new government. They were not convinced that the government would provide significant protections for themselves and their families. Although they were considerably smaller in size, these groups were much like today's guerrillas who insist on a comprehensive peace plan that goes beyond the simple decommissioning of weapons and the reinsertion into civilian life. The forces in this region were raising the issues of land and political reform as essential components of any agreement with the government. Anything else constituted unconditional surrender. These guerrillas provided the backbone of what became known as the "Independent Republics," scattered across the jungles of the Andean foothills and organized as communities of military self-defense and economic self-management. Naturally, their position was not greeted favorably by the government.

Pressured by wealthy landowners who had been forced to leave during the first phase of *La Violencia* and who were now demanding a return to their large landholdings, Rojas spearheaded operations against these agrarian guerrillas. The counterguerrilla offensive against these armed holdouts was carried out with the support of the United States. Hundreds of peasants were killed by the army in what became known as a "Military Operations Zone" in Sumapáz, leading to even more displacement. Gonzalo Sánchez described it best when he wrote: "Pacification once more came to be a synonym for devastation, machine-gunning, and bombardment. At least six battalions, around one-third of the Army's total force, were involved, supported by a torture center known during the era as the concentration camp of Cunday."[10]

As has been the case throughout the history of Colombia's internal conflict, civilians bore the brunt of the cost of this attack. The unexpected resistance to this systematic state-sponsored terror continued, however, and provided the seeds for today's guerrilla movement. Again, the historical parallels between that period and today are stunning, which is why it is not surprising that human rights activists are so quick to sound alarm bells when President Alvaro Uribe justifies the creation of "Zonas de rehabilitación," or zones of rehabilitation, currently controlled by the armed forces in high-conflict areas of the country with total military, judicial, and political control, while limiting access to the areas to journalists and other outsiders. Indeed, this approach has been used by many presidents in the last forty years as they have tried to confront the guerrilla threat militarily, with very little success.

The fact is that General Rojas Pinilla did carry out "rehabilitation" in certain parts of the country affected by *La*

Violencia, particularly in the newly colonized areas in the eastern plains where some government funds were directed. Nevertheless, this program had mixed results, not the least of which was the overt, ruthless violence that was being carried out in Sumapáz. Adding to the dangerous climate were the contradictory political moves that General Rojas Pinilla was making to appease both Liberals and Conservatives, to the detriment of truly democratic reform and justice for the victims of the first years of *La Violencia*. Although Liberal guerrillas were being amnestied, Conservative supporters of the exiled Gómez were being released from prison, committed to waging campaigns of reprisals against the former armed combatants, local Liberal leaders, and their perceived peasant supporters. Violence began to pick up again, and the two major parties blamed Rojas for being the primary cause, obscuring the fact that they had been complicit in the violence in defense of their own economic and political interests.

Within two years of the coup that was meant to bring peace and reconciliation to the country, Liberals and Conservatives began to realize that the government's amnesty was at best a political move to consolidate its power and, ironically, build a so-called third force to challenge the traditional elite power structure. In other words, their political duopoly was now being threatened by a military man they had initially endorsed. It soon became apparent that he was no longer needed. By 1957, General Rojas Pinilla was forced to step down by a powerful alliance of Conservative backers of former president Gómez, the Liberal Party establishment, and the armed forces. The result was what became known as the National Front. It was a mutually agreed upon political arrangement guaranteeing that political control of the country would remain in the hands of the two traditional parties for the foreseeable future. The two parties would rotate control of the presidency every four years for the next twenty years. They would share the spoils of local and departmental political offices. Colombia's oligarchy, while giving lip service to supporting democratic reform, could rest easy knowing that their interests would be adequately served by both parties. The fascist Gómez, forced to flee in disgrace a few years earlier, returned to Colombia vindicated after a brief period in exile. The National Front was born with very little hope for truly democratic opening and with a brewing peasant insurgency that saw itself increasingly isolated from this constitutional marriage within the oligarchy. The deep-rooted social problems that sprang from the question of unequal land distribution had not been resolved. A government-led wave of repression fully supported by the United States and characterized by violent expulsions against the peasant "self-defense" communities was launched, fueling further displacement, colonization, and changes in rural land tenure favorable to large landowners. Although the establishment of the National Front is often presented as the official end of *La Violencia*, a new, more troubling phase in the violence was now being launched that would shape Colombian reality for the next forty-five years (and beyond).

II

The Principal Actors
in Today's Conflict

3

The Contemporary Guerrilla Movement

It would be unfair to talk about *one* guerrilla movement in Colombia. It would be more accurate to describe a number of guerrilla movements with distinct historical roots, diverging political ideologies, and a broad array of clandestine and non-clandestine strategies to challenge the Colombian government.[1] But for the purposes of trying to understand the contemporary conflict and the solutions that are being proposed by the current governments in Washington and Bogotá, it makes sense to look specifically at the Revolutionary Armed Forces of Colombia, or FARC, one of the first groups that emerged in the National Front context as a direct response to the official violence and militarist aggression outlined in the previous chapter.

The FARC came into being on July 20, 1964 (Colombia's Independence Day), when groups of militants from the regions affected by the brutal, United States–backed military offensives of the previous years got together and issued their agrarian program. The Conference of the Southern Bloc included members of the group that survived the attacks on the now legendary Marquetalia, led by Manuel Marulanda Vélez, alias *Tirofijo* or "Sureshot," as well as other regions of southern and eastern Tolima. The conference issued its political military declaration as a way to consolidate its actions with a view towards the future:

We are revolutionaries struggling for a change in regime. But we always wanted and struggled for this change for our people using the least painful means: through peaceful means, through the democratic struggle of the masses, through the legal mechanism spelled out in the Colombian Constitution. This path was closed to us violently, and since we are revolutionaries that in one way or another are going to play the historic role that corresponds to us, we have been forced to find another way: the path of armed revolution for the struggle for power.[2]

Originally made up of Liberal guerrillas, the peasant founders of the FARC also included followers of the Colombian Communist Party, although the organization was not a military wing of the party. The Colombian Communist Party was perceived to be pro-Moscow, but the FARC by no means represented a transplanted, externally influenced insurrection, as the U.S. government had at times tried to convey. This argument allowed Washington to promote its own agenda in Colombia. In fact, the Colombian government's response to the "independent republics" was seen as a "continental response" that came from outside of the country in order to advance a strategy that was sympathetic to President John F. Kennedy's Alliance for Progress, a history that has been fully documented both in Colombia and elsewhere.[3] Rather than seeing the rebels as an organic manifestation of resistance to an extremely militarist and undemocratic system, the United States was quick to place it within the context of the recent triumph of the Cuban Revolution and the perceived threats in the hemisphere from the Soviet Union. Here again the parallels with contemporary Colombia are stunning when we consider Bush administration claims that Al Qaeda cells are operating in guerrilla strongholds along the Colombia-

Ecuador border, or that the FARC has links with groups such as the Hezbollah, accusations reported in recent news reports, details of which we will discuss in chapter 6. As in the 1960s, today, a local response must fit into a global response.

The early founders of the FARC were well aware of the fact that they were confronting a very powerful enemy in the Colombian army and its backers in Washington, forcing them from the beginning to carry out "political work with the masses in a grand scale" that would be done not only in areas where the original rebels were situated but also elsewhere as they expanded their movement. They were conscious of the need to develop ways of financing the movement through the direct support of the communities, as well as implementing education and propaganda efforts into regions where guerrillas had never existed. Immediately, the young rebels wanted to demonstrate to the Colombian public that they were not defeated, and that in fact the military offensives in Marquetalia against the peasant guerrillas actually strengthened them as an organization.[4]

Other guerrilla groups also emerged during this period, including the National Liberation Army, or ELN, a Cuban-inspired movement founded in 1965 in stretches of the Middle Magdalena Valley in the northeastern department of Santander. The ELN was not a genuine peasant movement like the FARC but drew its base of support from disaffected middle-class youth. Its ideological formation came from a revolutionary brand of liberation theology personified by one of its most famous recruits, Camilo Torres, killed in combat in 1966. Much smaller than the FARC, the ELN was almost wiped out in the early 1970s and resurged later under the leadership of the radical Spanish priest Manuel Pérez, or "Cura Pérez," who was seen as the key person responsible for refocusing the ELN into a politico-military organization in the early 1980s. Today the ELN numbers about 2,000 to 3,000 combatants; it is most known for its tactic of blowing up oil pipelines throughout the country as a way to confront the generous oil concessions given to foreign oil companies, which they see as a surrender of the national patrimony. These pipeline explosions have been criticized by environmental groups within Colombia and are the target of the $98 million training program involving U.S. Special Forces and Colombia's army in the northeastern department of Arauca. The ELN continues to maintain a level of stiff resistance against the state, but nowhere near the level of the FARC. Some observers initially thought the government of President Alvaro Uribe would use the ELN as a political tool in its war against the FARC by conducting limited peace talks with the smaller organization in order to demonstrate to the world that his government is serious about negotiating with left-wing guerrillas, all the while waging an aggressive military strategy against the FARC. In the first year of Uribe's mandate, however, this analysis has proven false, as the government has targeted both the FARC and ELN with equal vigor.

The Popular Liberation Army (EPL), was the armed wing of the Communist Party-Marxist Leninist (PC-ML). It emerged in 1967 in the peasant communities of Alto Sinú in the department of Córdoba, as well as other areas of Colombia's northwest. A number of factors led to its gradual demise, not the least of which was internal divisions over political and military strategy, and direct military repression against the communities from which its members came. Territorial battles between the FARC and EPL also took quite a toll, leading some members of the EPL to later take up sides with right-wing paramilitaries confronting the FARC in Urabá in the 1990s.

Another group, the M-19 (Movimiento 19 de Abril), takes its name from the date, April 19, 1970, when General Rojas Pinilla, through the political group he had founded six years earlier known as the National Popular Alliance (ANAPO), was blatantly robbed of an election by the National Front power structure and its presidential candidate Misaél Pastrana (the father of former president Andres Pastrana). For the ANAPO leadership, the stolen election was a clear message that political pluralism was indeed a myth in Colombia and the only option was an armed response. The M-19 was primarily an urban-based guerrilla movement without a real agrarian program that was officially launched in 1972 with members of ANAPO and former FARC leaders who were convinced that the FARC's was a struggle for land and not for state power. The organization specialized in high-profile assaults described by some as military publicity stunts lacking any cohesive, long-term, national, political vision. Because of these actions, the M-19 generated considerably more public attention than the FARC in the 1980s, the most spectacular event being the siege of the Palace of Justice in 1985, resulting in the deaths of the entire Colombian Supreme Court and countless others after the military stormed the building in a reckless "rescue attempt."[5] In 1991 the M-19 signed a peace treaty with the Colombian government, sending delegates to the National Constituent Assembly and gaining a number of seats in the Congress, in local municipalities, and in other elected offices. Dozens of M-19 militants were assassinated before and even after signing the peace accords, the victims of what human rights groups describe as the "dirty war" carried out against trade unionists, social activists, and members of the political left since the early 1980s. Today the political relevance of the M-19 as a national movement is practically nonexistent, although a number of its most visible former leaders continue to play a role in the political opposition to President Uribe.

Of these guerrilla organizations—ELN, EPL, and M-19—only the ELN still maintains some influence militarily, although it too has lost considerable power over the years. None of them, nor the many other guerrilla factions and offshoots that have emerged in Colombia over the years,[6] compare to the FARC in terms of its size, territorial influence, or military power.

The Gradual Growth of the FARC

In the 1970s, the FARC was a somewhat limited force with marginal military capacity, operating about nine fronts with what some observers have described as "enormous internal divisions."[7] It was not until the 1980s that the FARC began to generate its highest levels of social and political support, a direct result of the mounting evidence that the Colombian political system was not open for everybody. Even after the National Front arrangement was finally removed in 1978, the ruling parties refused to make meaningful changes in the way politics was conducted. As historian David Bushnell writes, this "confirmed the beliefs of all who had insisted that only armed force could make a difference."[8] The growth and strength of the guerrillas at the time, therefore, cannot be attributed solely to the expansion of the drug trade in Colombia, as many Colombian officials often argue in their attempts to depoliticize them. The relationship between the FARC and the illicit drug trade is one that is very complex, having evolved considerably over the years. Although there is no question that their reliance on drug money has contributed to their growing military strength, one cannot ignore the political factors behind this growth.

On several occasions over the past three decades, political opposition groups have tried to organize through legitimate means, only to get exterminated by state and parastate forces; the M-19 was one such group, but the gravest example was the Patriotic Union (UP), a political party established by the FARC in 1984 in an effort to engage in legal political activity. At the time, the FARC was engaged in peace negotiations with then president Belisario Betancur. President Betancur was trying to reverse four years of escalating military conflict and repression that was ruthlessly carried out by his predecessor, Julio Cesar Turbay Ayala. In the early to mid-1980s, the FARC was reconsidering its national strategy, maintaining a strong and growing presence in the countryside, but also incorporating a push into the cities through political action. The Patriotic Union represented that push.

The UP was made up of some of the most articulate voices and brilliant political minds of the Colombian left. Included in its ranks were progressive activists and intellectuals from the Communist Party, as well as the traditional parties, local and regional social movements, and the guerrilla movement itself and its support base. Despite winning seats in dozens of local, municipal, and departmental bodies, the traditional oligarchy and the military refused to let them truly participate in political life. In ten years, the UP lost 3,000 of its militants to the dirty war, including two presidential candidates. Threats, assassinations, and general intimidation was the price for trying to establish a legitimate, third political force, lending credence to the ongoing argument of the armed resistance that there are no guarantees for truly independent voices in Colombia. For the last several years, the Colombian human rights nongovernmental organization *Reiniciar* has been working within the structures of the Inter-American Commission of Human Rights of the Organization of American States to classify the extermination of the UP as genocide carried out by organisms of the state, a campaign that has received little attention in the Colombian media. While the tens of thousands of people affected by this dark episode in Colombian "democracy" are not quick to forget, the powers that be prefer to file it away into the archive of collective amnesia. For the FARC, it was a clear lesson. By the end of the 1980s it became apparent that peace talks from the government's standpoint were designed to simply disarm the rebels and not resolve the longstanding issues that led the rebels to take up arms in the first place.

In fact, the FARC's increasing focus on a military as opposed to a political strategy in the past decade—something that has lost the organization considerable support over the years from progressive circles within Colombia—can be tied directly to the dirty war against the UP and the failure of the state to provide guarantees for those militants who attempted to partake in civilian political life. The guerrillas justify the expansion of their military program as the only means to force the government to truly carry out structural reforms that go beyond the superficiality of including decommissioned combatants in the cabinet or in the legislature, something that was tried in the past with other sectors of the armed opposition like the M-19, a small faction of the ELN, as well as the EPL, with very little to show for in terms of a truly democratic transformation.

There is no question that the guerrillas should be criticized for their ongoing use of kidnapping of civilians as a deliberate tactic in their war against the state, for their incursions into indigenous communities and threats against indigenous leaders, for their intimidation and assassinations of local elected officials throughout the country, and for their indiscriminate attacks on civilians, both in the heat of battle and in high-profile actions carried out in the cities. Many, if not all, of these actions can indeed be considered terrorist in the traditional sense, particularly because of their impact on civilians. However, it is difficult to argue against the guerrillas' position regarding democratic guarantees for demobilized combatants given the historical track record of the Colombian government in the wake of previous peace accords with other armed groups. In this sense, their role as an armed opposition force cannot be negated, notwithstanding Uribe's (and many others') claims that they are terrorists or criminals.

The level of social disintegration that existed in Colombia in the 1980s was exacerbated by the expansion of the drug trade, and in particular the power of the Medellín cartel headed by Pablo Escobar. Indeed, it was this aspect of Colombia's internal crisis that received the most attention in the United States and elsewhere at the time. Meanwhile, the corruption, the never-ending civil war, and the violence against political and social movements reached a boiling point toward the end of the decade and into the 1990s. It must be noted that the intensification of the domestic sociopolitical crisis coincided with historic, global developments such as the end of the Cold War and the expansion of the neoliberal economic program throughout the Western Hemisphere. It was widely recognized within Colombia that the state needed to be modernized in order to fit into the new global order that was emerging, a modernization process that recognized the importance of dialogue in creating a social, political, and cultural community. Ironically, that process also included the dismantling of many of the state programs and institutions that were designed to protect the population.

As mentioned earlier, new sets of peace talks were held among the government and the M-19, the EPL, a small faction of the ELN, and the indigenous rebel group Armed Movement Quitin Lame (MQL). A dialogue was also underway with the FARC, but the talks eventually went nowhere, the result of the ongoing mistrust over the attacks on the UP and military assaults on FARC strongholds. As it turned out, notwithstanding the cautious optimism that was developing with respect to the limited peace overtures, Colombia was far from resolving its armed conflict.

The New Constitution and Its Impact on the Guerrillas

The peace talks in 1989–1990 led to the Constituent Assembly that was mandated to rewrite the antiquated Constitution of 1886. The new Constitution was drafted by a broad cross section of Colombian society that included indigenous leaders, former guerrillas, businessmen, and traditional as well as independent politicians. This was an attempt to correct the many contradictions described earlier, and it was widely seen as resulting from years of organized popular resistance—armed and "legal"—to a very authoritarian, undemocratic system that based its legitimacy on the veneer of a constitutional democracy.

The inclusion of indigenous representatives in the Constituent Assembly must be seen as a watershed moment in the history of Colombia's social movements and democratic opposition in general, and it directly affected public perceptions about the guerrilla movement. Indeed, to a certain extent, the success of the indigenous organizations demonstrated to Colombians of all political stripes that a social movement outside the traditional political party system and autonomous of the armed opposition could gain political space within Colombia. Some observers have criticized the various indigenous organizations—the National Indigenous Organization of Colombia (ONIC), Indigenous Social Alliance (ASI), Indigenous Authorities of Colombia (AICO), and the many regional organizations—of being too focused on the rights and struggles of their own people, in a sense being special-interest groups representing a small minority of the population and not concerned with the societal transforming processes of the broader popular movements. Yet this criticism is shortsighted and does not take into account the many alliances spearheaded by the indigenous leadership on a regional and national level. This criticism also underestimates the significance of what the indigenous movement accomplished in 1991, forcing the entire nation to recognize for the first time that Colombia is indeed a multiethnic, pluricultural society in which every person is of equal value and warrants the same protections regardless of their ethnic or racial background. That this constitutional progress was achieved forced the broader popular social movements to recognize that, notwithstanding the risks and the limitations, perhaps there was another way to achieve certain political gains that did not involve the use of armed struggle. Furthermore and perhaps more important, the limited gains of the indigenous movement directly challenged the FARC who, in the process of creating a revolutionary "sub-state" in their areas of control, saw indigenous demands for autonomy, land, and cultural rights as inherently counterrevolutionary. These tensions have remained ever since, and in some cases have gotten worse.

The 1990s saw a rapid change in the fundamental nature of the guerrilla struggle. When peace talks between the FARC and the government of Cesar Gaviria collapsed, the response from the government once again was "total war," based on the faulty premise that the rebels could be contained militarily without addressing the root causes that brought them into the conflict in the first place. As time went on, it became apparent that the "democratic guarantees" spelled out in the new Constitution were not worth the paper they were written on, as political murders, disappearances, and other human rights abuses continued against the popular movement, unabated. The brutal massacre of twenty Páez Indians on December 16, 1991, by gunmen linked to the local police in the municipality of Santander de Quilichao in the department of Cauca sent a chill to all popular sectors. To a certain extent, the FARC's refusal to surrender its weapons was vindicated, although it led directly to a new escalation in the conflict.

To begin with, paramilitary violence financed by large drug traffickers and coordinated with the armed forces began to pick up, with the primary targets being peasants, trade unionists, and leftist political and social organizations throughout the country. With a heightened level of U.S. intervention developing in the name of the war on drugs, the FARC was forced to adjust its guerrilla tactics at the local level in order to increase revenues for funding its war against the state. The political project that they had proposed in the 1980s quickly faded, overtaken by an expansive military strategy. This led to an increase in the use of kidnapping and extortion of the civilian population, which gradually began to lose the FARC the public support it had cultivated a decade earlier.

Finally, the complex relationship between the FARC and the illicit drug trade began to evolve beyond the rebel's daily contacts with the poor peasant farmers that cultivate coca in regions where the guerrillas had situated themselves years earlier in the vacuum left by the state. Much like the financial demands made on cattle ranchers, banana growers, and the oil industry in other parts of the country, the guerrillas initially levied so-called war taxes on farmers, merchants, and groups operating the processing labs and airstrips used for cocaine shipments in coca-growing regions. Over the years, however, the FARC has penetrated even deeper into the drug business, now directly overseeing these and other aspects of the trade, thereby generating much more income.[9]

In this sense, FARC is perceived as both a defender and a danger to the peasant farmers who cultivate coca as their primary means of economic activity. Guerrillas have sided with the farmers over the issue of the government's toxic aerial eradication campaign, demanding development alternatives for the regions most affected and an end to the United States–backed fumigations. In many parts of the country, the FARC has also served as the "local authority," providing security and "revolutionary justice" for the local peasant communities, resolving everything from traffic violations to domestic disputes.

At the same time, the FARC is also known to apply considerable pressure on the campesinos of Putumayo, Guaviare, Caquetá, Cauca and elsewhere, not only in terms of their participation in coca cultivation, but also in terms of demanding food, transportation, and other logistical support to the rebels.

I remember once, while driving in the SUV of an indigenous *cabildo* (council) in southern Cauca, we were stopped by four FARC guerrillas who demanded a ride to the nearest town. The driver of the vehicle refused, saying the car was owned by the cabildo and they had no reason to get involved in the guerrillas' activities. His refusal was risky but was buttressed by the fact that a well-known indigenous leader who was in the car with us took the lead in explaining why they wouldn't give the guerrillas a ride. Peasants from other communities under similar circumstances would not have had the audacity to reject the guerrillas' demand. One of the unfortunate byproducts of this type of relationship is that peasants are put in harm's way because the army and their paramilitary allies target them as willing collaborators with the insurgency. At the same time, any local leader or group that attempts to construct an autonomous organization or present a neutral position vis-à-vis the conflict is seen as an enemy by the FARC, an enemy that very often must be liquidated.

Although they are far from being an international drug-trafficking organization similar to the Medellín or Cali cartels that were dismantled in the early to mid-1990s, it is no longer accurate to say the FARC's involvement in the drug trade remains limited to their imposition of a war tax on farmers. The amount of revenue generated by the FARC through its role in the drug trade is hard to measure. Indeed, it is still seen as a small percentage of the overall amounts of money exchanged globally in the international drug market. It pales in comparison to the money involved in the actual distribution and marketing of the finished product that is cocaine once it is exported. What is clear is that the FARC's military focus of the last ten to twelve years forced it to find more lucrative funding sources, with the illicit drug trade and kidnapping being two very important ones. The corrupting influence of drug money has penetrated just about every sector of Colombian society, including the armed forces and the political establishment. To argue that it has not had the same corrupting influence on certain elements of this large guerrilla army, as defenders of the FARC often claim, is to live in a state of naïve denial.

As this process unfolded, the FARC continued to grow: It has almost quadrupled in size in the last fifteen years, from roughly 3,600 combatants in 1987, to 7,000 in 1995, to today with estimates ranging between 15,000 and 20,000 fighters operating in more than 105 fronts with control of more than 40 percent of the national territory. Some people attribute this growth to the guerrillas' growing involvement in narcotrafficking. Others say it is the result of the forced recruitment carried out by the FARC in the countryside and has less to do with the personal ideological convictions of the new combatants. Perhaps the real answer lies in a socioeconomic crisis whereby most youth living in the countryside are for all intents and purposes unemployable in any legitimate productive sector. They have a choice either to look for work in the cities, where unemployment rates in recent years have reached as high as 22 percent, or to take up arms with one or another military organization, legal or otherwise. I've talked to dozens of people in remote parts of the Colombian countryside who, with considerable trepidation, admit that for them the FARC and the paramilitary groups are the two most stable employers of the region, guaranteeing them a salary, a uniform, regular meals, and, most tragically, a weapon.

As a result of this rapid growth, in the late 1990s the Colombian army was handed a series of humiliating military setbacks at the hands of the FARC, suffering numerous casualties throughout the country after a number of dramatic assaults on military installations and police stations. The FARC was able to capture dozens of soldiers and police officials in some of these operations, embarrassing the military and forcing the government not only to rethink its overall strategy but actually give in to a number of highly controversial guerrilla demands. The fact that the government of President Andres Pastrana demilitarized five municipalities in southern Colombia controlled by the FARC in January 1999 in order to jumpstart peace talks was a clear demonstration of the military successes of the guerrillas. Critics argued that the government's position in the talks was doomed from the start because it was negotiating from a position of strategic weakness. The growing consensus in Washington and Bogotá was that the military simply needed to get tougher.

Does the FARC Have a Political Platform?

Many people were critical of Pastrana's decision to cede the five municipalities to the FARC during the peace talks, an issue that received most of the attention of the media during the entire process. As a result, none of the guerrillas' political positions and proposals were given any serious consideration. The FARC as an insurgent movement does have a twelve-point political program made public for many years, but it is rarely presented in media reports about the war or in the debates about ways to resolve the war. Colombians who support President Uribe's tougher stand against the guerrillas and who opposed the peace talks started by Pastrana very often ask "What does the FARC want? They don't have a political vision anymore, they're just a bunch of bandits." Again, the language is designed to depoliticize the rebels. This view is due partly to the FARC's own failure to truly articulate its political platform while instead carrying out dozens of major military actions. But the confusion—or obfuscation—is also due to the Colombian media's overwhelming tendency to avoid presenting the insurgent's position objectively.

Some of the main points of the FARC's platform include a desire to find a political solution to the "grave conflict facing the country"; a comprehensive reform of the armed forces and national security apparatus in order to guarantee that the army will be used to defend the national borders and not be used against the Colombian people; direct, democratic participation in national, regional, and municipal decisions that "compromise the future of the society," an idea related to creating a new type of active, democratic citizenry; the modernization and development of the national economy with social justice as a primary concern; a more equitable tax structure that would force "those with more wealth to pay more taxes"; an agrarian policy that would "democratize credits, technical assistance and the marketing of products"; the exploitation of the country's natural resources to "benefit the nation and its regions"; and the development of international relations that respects the self-determination of peoples worldwide.[10]

Clearly some of these points may seem to be far-reaching, ambiguous, and perhaps even contradictory. But under different circumstances, they would provide interesting points of departure to begin thorough and open debates about the future direction of the country. Indeed, these ideas coincide with the platforms of a broad cross section of the popular social movements.

If it was difficult for the FARC leadership to convey its platform while peace talks with the government were going on, it has become next to impossible to convey even a fraction of these points during an intense, all-out war like the one that was launched after Uribe took power in August 2002. For much of 2003, the FARC was left responding to claims that it was gradually being weakened. All of these factors lend credence to the argument that the guerrillas are more comfortable in the battlefield than at the negotiating table. It is a perception fueled both by the general media blackout against the FARC's political objectives, and also by recent FARC actions carried out in the last several years as the conflict has deteriorated.

Abuses by the FARC

As we'll see in chapter 4, the tactic of using civilians as cannon fodder in its war against the "enemy" is used by every armed actor in the Colombian conflict, including the FARC. The FARC has been accused of carrying out massacres of civilians, assassinations of what they describe as paramilitary collaborators, and issuing threats against local officials and community leaders who are seen as being too closely tied to the state, including mayors, city council members, and representatives to departmental assemblies. The levels of intimidation and threats against civilian activists of all political persuasions make it very difficult to develop legitimate, independent institutions, especially in the countryside. This is not to mention the guerrillas' relentless use of kidnapping as a primary funding source for its insurgency. Guerrillas are linked to more than 1,700 kidnappings annually, and the number of people forcibly disappeared now averages five per day.[11]

All this has led to the alienation of the civilian population in many parts of the country and has contributed to the growing problem of internal displacement. One example occurred in May 2001, when the FARC killed as many as twenty-four farmers in several towns in the municipality of Tierralta, in the northern department of Córdoba. According to human rights groups, twelve of the victims were decapitated. Hundreds of residents fled their homes as a result.[12] A more recent attack occurred in the town of Bellavista, Bojayá, in the northwestern department of Chocó, on May 2, 2002. In the incident, 119 people, including 45 children, were killed when a FARC cylinder mortar struck a rural church where inhabitants had sought refuge during a guerrilla-paramilitary battle. An independent review found that the army (for failing to protect the town), the paramilitaries (for using the civilians as human shields), and the guerrillas (for bombing the church), all must be held accountable for the events of this particular tragedy. Although the FARC acknowledged it as an "accident," the bombing points to the destructive nature of their reckless use of these types of rudimentary weapons in civilian areas.

Over the years, the FARC has threatened and assassinated prominent leaders of indigenous communities who challenged guerrilla incursions into their territories or who took exception to the forced recruitment of indigenous youth by guerrillas. According to the Indigenous Organization of Antióquia (OIA), one of the most influential regional indigenous groups in Colombia, between September 1986 and August 2001 the FARC was responsible for twenty-seven assassinations; fifteen direct threats; and fourteen other cases of occupation, dislocation, detention, or forced work of indigenous community members in that department alone. These numbers are duplicated in other parts of the country with large numbers of indigenous people.[13] The brutal and senseless murder by FARC combatants in March 1999 of three United States–based indigenous rights activists who had been working with the U'Wa people in their struggle against Occidental Petroleum was highly publicized and universally denounced. Although it did not lead to the forced displacement of the U'Wa, it aggravated an already dangerous climate in the area that was threatening the 6,000-member indigenous community. The murders puzzled many and disgusted even more: How could a group claiming to be "the People's Army" carry out such a horrendous act against three unarmed civilians who were carrying out work in defense of the U'Wa as they confronted a major United States–based transnational oil company? The murders contributed to Washington's stepped-up pressure on the Pastrana administration to play hardball with the guerrillas, making the unfolding efforts at peace talks with the FARC that much more difficult. These types of violent acts lend credence to the argument that the FARC has lost its political direction by spending too much time carrying out military actions, many of which could be considered outright criminal.

The fact is that the FARC has witnessed a profound evolution as an organization in their forty years of existence. Just as the FARC of 1964 was very different in terms of its political focus and military capacity than the FARC of 1984, it is obvious that the FARC today is very different from what it represented twenty years ago. It once maintained considerable legitimacy and support within the peasantry and represented their interests as a political and military group. Today that support has decreased considerably for a number of the reasons already outlined, not the least of which has been the growth of the right-wing paramilitary groups in areas where the FARC traditionally operated with relative free reign.

Other factors impacted this evolution. The total war launched by the Gaviria administration in the early 1990s forced the guerrilla leadership to rethink its military command structure. The guerrillas began to move away from the rigid top-down bureaucracy to one more dependent on a system of regional blocs and fronts operating throughout the country. In a sense this made it a much more efficient and formidable strategic-military rival for the government, but also made these units much more independent and less accountable. Furthermore, the failure of the Gaviria administration to implement the democratic reforms stipulated in the 1991 Constitution exacerbated the problem of governability and legitimacy that the FARC, for better or for worse, was able to exploit. And finally, the rapid growth of coca cultivation in areas of peasant colonization traditionally controlled by the FARC resulted in two things: First, it created even stronger enemies for the FARC in the form of the major narcotraffickers linked to paramilitaries who saw the guerrillas as encroaching in their interests; and second, as has already been pointed out, coca provided the FARC with an important revenue stream that enabled them to fortify their military machine.

Although it would have been extremely naïve to think that these developments were going to lead to the first successful peasant revolution since the Vietnam War, as some leftist scholars were articulating in the mid-1990s, the situation that was unfolding was the perfect formula for a prolonged, intensified, and bloody civil war for the years to come. The FARC's demands of no more aerial fumigations in the south, of a transformation of the neoliberal economic program that devastated the agricultural and small business sectors, of an overhaul of the military and security apparatus, and of an end to further U.S. intervention all became irrelevant against the backdrop of its aggressive military tactics. Similar demands being put forward by the popular movement were thereby systematically ignored.

Can the FARC Be Defeated?

Colombia reached a strategic stalemate many years ago, and the belief that an expansion of military power will lead to the defeat of the guerrillas is a dangerous proposition expressed by the most hawkish elements in both the Colombian and U.S. governments. Some make the case that the Uribe-Bush hardline strategy is designed to beat down the guerrillas enough in order to set the stage for future peace talks whereby the government would be negotiating from a position of strength, thus forcing the guerrillas to make concessions that in previous talks they were unwilling to make. The only way to do this, they argue, is to expand the military budget and beef up the armed forces with better hardware, more effective training, and draconian internal security measures.

On the surface, this argument makes sense, considering the levels of insecurity that exist in Colombia and the degree to which the guerrillas contribute to this insecurity. As I have described in this chapter, the FARC, the ELN, and several other armed guerrilla factions have been waging a protracted war on Colombian security personnel, sectors of the civilian population, and vital national infrastructure for four decades. Regardless of whether or not their actions are justifiable, one would be hard pressed to argue that the government does not have the responsibility to establish legal control within its own national territory in order to protect and defend the citizenry. Again and again, Colombians point to the issue of security as one of their top priorities, so one would expect elected officials and their security personnel to respond accordingly. This has been the primary argument raised by President Uribe.

At the same time, it is extremely shortsighted to think that strengthening the military is going to lead to that control, let alone create the conditions that are favorable to peace negotiations. Indeed, given the track record of the Colombian armed forces, there is little reason to believe that their fortification is going to lead to a fundamental sense of long-term security for the majority of the Colombian population. The military victory that many hawks within the Colombian armed forces believe to be possible should not be expected either. For example, in May 2003, two top government officials criticized Uribe's beefed-up military strategy for failing to stem the flow of violence in the oil-producing region of Arauca, a so-called Rehabilitation and Consolidation Zone. Inspector General Edgardo Maya and government Human Rights Ombudsman Eduardo Cifuentes issued reports that found that violence and insecurity, as well as violations of human rights, were actually increasing in Arauca despite the increased powers given to military authorities since September 2002.[14]

In August 2002, when Uribe was inaugurated as the get-tough president, his vice president, Francisco Santos, described the U.S.

congressional authorization to apply more than $1.7 billion in counterdrug aid against the guerrillas for counterinsurgency purposes as essential in helping "to change the military balance . . . to contain the violent ones."[15] Defense Minister Martha Lucía Ramírez told the Associated Press in January 2003 that with enough U.S. military aid, stronger security forces funded by Uribe's 1.2 percent war tax, and citizen informants situated around the country, they could weaken the rebels enough to allow the government "to gain control of every part of the country."[16] When the National Assembly of Bishops, in its annual gathering in Bogotá in July 2003, called on all sides to negotiate a solution to the conflict, General Jorge Enrique Mora, commander of the armed forces, responded by saying that another viable option was "winning this war on the battlefield."[17] What Santos, Ramírez, and Mora failed to point out is that the FARC would find ways to counter this new "firepower" provided by the United States, as it has done in the past. It's almost as if history were repeating itself.

The high command of the FARC often attribute their early radicalization in the 1960s to the interventionism of the United States. They point to Washington's counterinsurgency containment policies that were applied directly against the early guerrillas' so-called Independent Republics during the first National Front government, described briefly in chapter 3. Raul Reyes, a member of the FARC's secretariat and one of its chief spokespersons, told me in an interview in 1996, echoing similar comments made years before by the FARC's commander in chief Manuel Marulanda Vélez, that had the Colombian government at the time "truly implemented fundamental land reform and political reform in the 1950s and '60s instead of opting for military solutions to address our grievances, the FARC would not exist today."[18]

Although this interpretation warrants more thorough historical review, recent developments tell us that stepped-up military attacks against the FARC may actually backfire. Unlike the smaller and weaker ELN—which is much more likely to succumb to the military offensive of the Bush-backed Uribe administration—the FARC will continue to resist U.S. interventionism at whatever cost, regardless of how many guerrillas surrender or are killed, captured, or even extradited. Between the months of June and August 2003, on an almost daily basis, the Colombian news media were flooded with reports of guerrilla desertions and captures. The government kept publicizing numbers showing how within one year it had made historic progress toward winning the war, citing the capture of 2,000 combatants and the deaths of more than 1,000 in direct combat. Commentators in Colombia's major media were openly saying that the FARC was losing the war.[19] Meanwhile, the FARC was sending different messages, denying in public statements that the military offensive of the Uribe government was having any major impact.[20] Quite the contrary. Some military analysts described the period as a lull in the guerrillas' ongoing war, part of a cycle that had been repeated in the past but without any long-term impact. High-profile military actions will most likely resume in the foreseeable future, regardless of the limited gains reported by the government.

In fact, as the Uribe administration began to implement its Democratic Defense and Security Policy, the official strategy document that outlines the stepped-up war against the FARC, the response from the rebels has been ferocious: A car bomb attributed to the FARC rocked a Bogotá social club in February 2003, killing dozens of people (the FARC denied responsibility for this attack about three weeks later, saying that it was the work of the paramilitaries); on May 5, the FARC executed ten hostages it had been holding, including former defense minister Gilberto Echeverri and a provincial governor, Guillermo Gaviria, during a botched rescue attempt by U.S.-trained commandos, an act later described by FARC leader Raul Reyes as "lamentable." In addition, there have been repeated attacks against police installations in different parts of the country, and three American intelligence contractors whose plane crashed in one of the FARC's southern Colombia strongholds were captured. All these actions were clear signals that the guerrillas were not giving in so easily. They were not in retreat, and the security so much desired by the Colombian people was not forthcoming.

In this regard, some analysts began saying the Bush-Uribe strategy may actually lead to the unintended consequences of forcing the FARC to depend even more on revenues generated from the drug trade than it already does because it is the only truly effective funding source for an adequate military counteroffensive. Not only does this expand the war on the military front, it provides fuel to the fire of the drug economy. And it of course raises the potential for the loss of more civilian lives. As was the case with the attacks against the "Independent Republics" in the 1960s, President Turbay-Ayala's brutal offensive against the FARC in the early 1980s, and President Gaviria's "total war" of the early 1990s, all supported unconditionally by the White House occupants at the time, the Uribe strategy is simply leading to a further escalation of the war, with no end in sight.

Despite their serious political contradictions, growing involvement in the drug trade, and destructive military tactics, the FARC must be seen as a political-military actor that will not go away simply by applying more military force. The military approach has failed repeatedly over the last forty years to the detriment of the entire Colombian population, primarily the poor and the most marginalized sectors. Today, to advocate any degree of compromise with the FARC is felt to be almost treasonous, considering the broad popular support that Uribe has generated for his get-tough posture, alongside the general disgust that people have towards the guerrillas, in particular the middle and upper classes. Just ask James LeMoyne, the UN Special Envoy to Colombia, who was accused by Colombia's Defense Minister Ramírez of "defending the interests of terrorists" after telling the newspaper *El Espectador* that, despite the FARC's criminal activity, many of its combatants still "maintain ideological convictions."[21] While LeMoyne pointed out that he was not taking sides but trying to encourage negotiations, Colombian officialdom was quick to say "we must end the debate" about the guerrillas, the only solution worthy of pursuing being all-out military confrontation.

A negotiated solution to Colombia's conflict is the only viable route, regardless of how long it might take or how unpopular this notion may be in today's climate, both within Colombia and on an international level. Ideally peace talks should be carried out under a comprehensive and verifiable cease-fire recognized by all sides in the conflict, although making it a condition for talks is not the best way to get to the negotiating table.

International mediation and verification may also be needed, in particular from the United Nations, something President Uribe suggested during his inaugural address and throughout the first part of his mandate, although it was later rejected by the FARC, which preferred direct talks with the government. The FARC was not opposed to UN participation as an observer body but was against having it serve as primary mediator, arguing that the government needed to negotiate directly with the FARC. This was especially significant because demobilization talks between the right-wing paramilitaries and the government were not preconditioned on UN mediation, an issue I will address in chapter 4.

Nevertheless, by the middle of 2003, the United Nations began to take on a more active role in helping to resolve the conflict. Ironically, at the same time, Uribe became increasingly critical of the institution, echoing the undiplomatic language used by President Bush to describe the Security Council during the debates leading up to the war in Iraq. Specifically, Uribe took exception to the UN recognition of the FARC as a belligerent force and its persistent push to encourage peace negotiations. In a June 2003 speech before the Interamerican Court for Human Rights in San José, Costa Rica, Uribe said bluntly: "The role we Colombians see the UN has been playing is that it criticizes a lot but resolves very little. I ask the UN to stop criticizing, and commit itself to resolving."[22] Like his counterpart in Washington, Uribe appreciates the UN only when it sees things his way.[23]

Perhaps most important, there is no question that any peace process must include those progressive sectors of civil society that do not feel represented by either the government or the guerrillas. Indeed, talks to end the conflict should incorporate the many demands being put forward by a broad cross-section of the peace movement—human rights groups, academics, trade union activists, indigenous and peasant communities, Afro-Colombians, the displaced—all of whom have been for the most part excluded from conversations between the government and leftist rebels. In the past, these groups were seen as divided, representing divergent interests that could not put up a unified front or movement. In recent years, as the situation deteriorated and as government forces, paramilitaries, and guerrillas escalated their violent actions, the civilian popular movement has found common ground in their collective struggles against militarism, neoliberalism, and interventionism. Their voices are very often silenced, either by threats and intimidation or by direct attack. Although they are by no means in complete agreement on many of the fundamental questions facing Colombia, somehow they must be included in any future dialogue.

Yet to say all of this does not negate the important and fundamental role that the armed insurgency must play in the long and delicate process of national reconciliation. The growing tendency of the government of Uribe and his backers in the White House to simply brand them as narcoterrorists does nothing to move this peace process forward and ignores the origins of their insurgency, thereby perpetuating the same failed policies of the past but perhaps to greater extremes.

The bottom line is that even if the FARC (and ELN) were to be militarily defeated on the battlefield tomorrow, a highly unlikely proposition, other armed opposition forces most likely will emerge as long as the political and economic power arrangement continues to be monopolized by the same groups. As Colombian scholar Ricardo Sánchez, former director of the Luís Carlos Galán Institute for the Development of Democracy, wrote: "The current political system cannot be maintained, one that rests on the hegemony of a few families, of political castes, that rests on the marriage between legal and illegal moneyed interests, between the powerful communications media and the Liberal and Conservative parties."[24] This is not to deny that there may be other motivating factors and interests driving the guerrillas' perceived intransigence in recent years, nor is this meant to rid the guerrillas of any responsibility for the deterioration of the current situation. It is more a reflection of the structural limitations of the Colombian political system, whose fundamental flaw is "the absence of alternatives that would provide channels for social protest," to quote Colombian philosopher Luis Alberto Restrepo.[25] However, the tendency of Colombian and U.S. policymakers to describe Colombia as a democracy under siege erases this reality from the debate about how to deal with the Colombia problem, and it allows for the promotion of primarily military solutions. Too often, those military solutions manifest themselves in terror tactics promoted by the state, as we'll see in the next chapter.

4

The "Paramilitaries" and the Dirty War

The decades-long guerrilla war in Colombia has been used as a smokescreen by a succession of governments to carry out systematic repression against the many individuals and organizations mobilizing for social, political, and economic change through legally recognized channels. By repeatedly branding these groups as "subversives," the Colombian military-political establishment has converted legally constituted social and political organizations, and the civilian population in general, into military targets themselves. In this respect, the presence of the guerrillas provides the state with the justification to declare states of emergency, suspend civil protections, expand the role of the military to include civilian police functions, endorse the use of torture, and wage a war against the popular movement, all the while failing to implement the political and economic reforms demanded by the vast majority of the population. Again and again, this is done in the name of national security, restoring order, and defending democracy.

When President Alvaro Uribe declared emergency powers in September 2002 that included the right to arrest and detain people without due cause, tap phone lines and enter homes without warrants, declare "rehabilitation and consolidation zones" totally under military control, and limit foreigners' access to conflict areas, he said it was to fight "terrorism" and confront the growing guerrilla threat. In Colombia, this has been unofficial policy for years and has been at the root of what human rights groups have described as the country's dirty war, manifested in countless cases of forced disappearances, summary executions, political assassinations, arbitrary detentions, and massacres of civilians. It's a situation that by all accounts has gotten worse since the late 1990s, a period that has also seen a radical increase in U.S. military assistance to and training in Colombia. The Colombian Commission of Jurists, for example, reports that the number of politically motivated deaths has increased from roughly ten per day in the early 1990s, to fourteen in 1999, to more than twenty per day in 2002.[1]

In the past, this systematic repression was carried out through official organisms of the state such as the armed forces, national police, and military intelligence. Over the years, however, after considerable criticism from international and domestic human rights organizations, the task of rooting out potential and actual "subversives" has been handed over to illegal paramilitary groups whose origins lie in the so-called self-defense militias created by drug traffickers and large landowners in the 1980s in areas where the guerrillas were carrying out kidnappings and other military operations, particularly in Urabá and Córdoba in northern Colombia.[2] It is no coincidence that this paramilitary phenomenon began to emerge as peace talks were taking place between then-president Belisario Betancur and various rebel factions in 1984, a process that was accompanied by widespread calls for democratization. At the time, the Colombian army began to arm civilians in order to curtail some of the political, and to a lesser extent military, gains of the guerrillas. It was a marriage of convenience between large landowners tied to narcotrafficking who were profoundly anticommunist and whose interests were threatened by guerrillas, and the Colombian military, thoroughly discredited as an institution for its high levels of corruption and complete failure to successfully confront the armed insurgency. As one Colombian analyst observed, it is also no coincidence that this happened during the tenure of Ambassador Lewis Tambs, President Reagan's representative in Colombia who coined the term *narcoguerrilla* in an effort to weaken the peace process underway with the insurgents. We must not forget that Tambs was the chief spokesperson in Colombia for an administration that had already established the unholy alliance of drug traffickers and Nicaraguan Contras in an effort to topple the Sandinistas.[3]

The results of this paramilitary enterprise have been documented extensively by human rights groups in Colombia and abroad. It is a phenomenon that has grown considerably in the last decade, and has moved from region to region throughout the country. Civilian massacres continued to rise in recent years, from 168 in 1999, to 236 in 2000, and 281 in 2001, the majority of them committed by members of the AUC—Autodefensas Unidas de Colombia, or United Self-Defense Forces of Colombia.[4] This in turn has led to the forced displacement of hundreds of thousands of civilians: An estimated 319,000 people were forced from their homes in 2000, 342,000 in 2001, and 350,000 in 2002, bringing the current total number to an estimated 2.75 million internally displaced people. This is not including the roughly 105,000–125,000 Colombians living in refugee-like conditions in neighboring countries.[5] In turn, the paramilitaries' capacity to implant stability and order in their regions of primary control has provided them with considerable support from the elite sectors of those regions, for years threatened by the guerrilla presence.[6]

Although it is easy to paint the displacement phenomenon as an unfortunate byproduct of a violent confrontation between the guerrillas and paramilitaries where civilians unfortunately get caught in the crossfire, a growing amount of evidence suggests the massacres of civilians are part of a deliberate strategy on the part of the right-wing AUC to take control of territory considered to be strategically valuable in relation to the broader economic interests of the sectors of Colombian society that the paramilitaries represent: large landowners, backers of so-called mega-projects, and, of course, narcotraffickers.[7] For the most part, the land being cleared just so happens to be territory considered to be traditional strongholds of the FARC or the ELN. As one displaced activist from the department of Chocó said to me, "it's simply a war about land and resources, and the people living in these lands happen to be in the way." Human rights groups and popular movement activists argue that paramilitaries have targeted not only civilians deemed "sympathetic to the guerrillas, but also whatever social, labor, popular, or peasant movement that happens to call to question the development of megaprojects" and the consolidation of economic interests that may not benefit their interests.[8]

Such is the case in the oil-refining town of Barrancabermeja in the northeastern department of Santander on the banks of the Magdalena River. For years the FARC and ELN maintained a strong presence around the perimeter of the town of roughly 220,000 inhabitants. In January 2001, the AUC began a campaign of terror in the area, killing 180 civilians in the city and dislodging roughly 4,000 residents, including thousands of women and children.[9] As a result of the paramilitary sweep, the AUC established a presence in a region through which much of the processed coca grown in surrounding areas must pass en route to the Caribbean as it makes its way to foreign markets. Barrancabermeja also happens to be a hotbed of union organizing, in particular the powerful oil workers union, the Unión Sindical de Obreros, or USO. For years USO has been challenging the government's generous oil concessions to multinational oil giants, carrying out work stoppages and other actions that have struck a chord on a national level as an example of popular resistance to foreign domination of Colombia's oil industry. As a result of this high-profile militancy, dozens of USO members have been killed, jailed, forcibly disappeared or threatened, accused of working hand in hand with the guerrillas of the ELN.

The actions carried out by the AUC in early 2001 were seen as the latest manifestation of years of repression of popular organizing in Barrancabermeja, particularly against the oil workers, their families, and supporters in other popular organizations. The acts of violence, threats, and intimidation continued for months thereafter, including attacks against a number of women's organizations whose members were placed on death lists. These attacks led to considerable national and international condemnation of the situation. It also sparked courageous and highly visible acts of civilian popular resistance and solidarity throughout 2001 and 2002, spearheaded primarily by the women of Barrancabermeja who, despite being under the watchful eye of paramilitary hit men, refused to be silenced or intimidated. As for bringing the perpetrators of the earlier massacres to justice, that's another less-inspiring story.

Indeed, the intensification of the war in the late 1990s and into 2002 led to "a noticeable decline in respect for human rights and international humanitarian law in Colombia" by all sectors in the conflict, as pointed out by the office of the United Nations High Commissioner for Human Rights (UNHCHR).[10] As described in chapter 3, the guerrillas should be held accountable for a portion of this escalating violence. However, the paramilitary organizations have deliberately chosen terror as their primary strategy of gaining territorial control of areas seen to be in the hands of the FARC and ELN. Very often this is done with complicit sectors of the Colombian armed forces, who themselves have wreaked terror throughout the countryside for decades.

Frankenstein's Monster:
Once a Paramilitary, Always a Paramilitary

In the 1980s, roughly 70 to 75 percent of all documented human rights violations carried out in Colombia were attributed to the armed forces and the national police. Today, the AUC is accused of up to 70 to 75 percent of these same crimes. In other words, the culpability ratio has shifted proportionally from the army to the paramilitaries (the guerrillas make up anywhere between 20 and 25 percent of all human rights violations, a poor record in and of itself). It is clear that, as human rights considerations climbed up the priority list of the U.S. foreign policy agenda, particularly in the Congress, the Colombian military was finding it increasingly difficult to come clean when it had its hand out seeking support from Washington. Human rights activists have argued it's not a coincidence that by the mid-1990s, the paramilitary organizations took over the role of primary human rights abusers as part of the government's overall counterinsurgency strategy. As a result, the Colombian army washed its hands of any responsibility for the human rights crisis facing Colombia while still benefiting from the paramilitary infrastructure that spread throughout the country. The process accelerated considerably in the mid-1990s. In 1996, Carlos Castaño, the political leader of the AUC, told Human Rights Watch that he commanded about 2,000 armed and trained fighters. By 2000, he claimed 11,200, an increase of 460 percent in four years, confirmed by the government's own statistics.[11] By 2003, when the government and the AUC were engaged in demobilization talks, the numbers of paramilitary combatants ranged from 13,000 to 19,500.

Despite the documented links between the AUC and the state security apparatus, in recent years Colombian authorities have publicly distanced themselves from the paramilitaries, describing them as terrorists who are also involved in drug trafficking. As Human Rights Watch reported in 2001, government officials ranging from the former attorney general's office to the public advocate had begun to take limited action against the paramilitaries, decommissioning officers accused of collaborating with death squads, seizing some weapons, and preventing some massacres. But "their actions have been consistently and effectively undermined, canceled out, or in some cases wholly reversed by actions promoted by the military-paramilitary alliance." Instead of concrete actions aimed at fundamentally altering the conditions on the ground, the government has "dedicated a great deal of energy and time to a public relations effort purporting to show that the military has made progress against paramilitaries."[12] By 2003, the Uribe government began to take more deliberate steps at capturing paramilitary fighters and decommissioning some of their weapons, presenting these actions as part of the administration's Democratic Defense and Security Policy aimed at re-establishing state authority throughout the country. For many human rights groups, however, these actions were cosmetic gestures carried out to obscure the gradual institutionalization of the paramilitary enterprise.[13] I will address this issue in greater detail later in this chapter.

U.S. Complicity in Paramilitarism

According to a number of nongovernmental human rights organizations, the United States has repeatedly ignored the Colombian government's failures to comply with the conditions placed on it for continued military assistance. The determination and certification for continued U.S. aid to the Colombian military in 2002 contained three primary conditions. The United States required the Colombian government "to suspend from the armed forces those members who have been credibly alleged to have committed gross violations of human rights"; to force the "full cooperation of the armed forces with civilian prosecutors and judicial authorities in prosecuting and punishing in civilian courts those members of the Colombian armed forces who have been credibly alleged to have committed gross violations of human rights"; and to make sure the "Colombian Armed Forces are taking effective measures to sever links . . . at the command, battalion, and brigade levels with paramilitary groups, and to execute outstanding orders for capture for members of such groups."[14]

In criticizing the 2002 State Department certification of Colombia that opened the door to more than $415 million in aid, Amnesty International, Human Rights Watch, and the Washington Office on Latin America pointed out that, for each condition, Colombia has not come clean. For example, the Colombian government has attempted to demonstrate its compliance with the first condition by citing the dismissal of hundreds of soldiers, which the State Department called a "step forward" in terms of accountability within the Colombian armed forces. But "the government has released no information to show that these individuals were dismissed because of involvement in human rights crimes and not other allegations like incompetence or sleeping on guard duty." As for the second condition, Colombia's armed forces continue to dispute the jurisdiction of cases involving the investigation and prosecution of alleged human rights violations by members of the military. Finally, and perhaps most important, both Colombian and international human rights groups continue to receive reports showing that "paramilitaries continue to operate with the acquiescence and support of the Colombian armed forces and have consolidated and in some areas expanded control." The report said it had become common for large paramilitary units to combat FARC units of equal size, very often assisted by government troops. Throughout Colombia, paramilitaries were able to move troops and supplies unhindered past military bases, roadblocks, troops, and check points.[15] Similar criticisms were levied at the State Department's certification of Colombia in July 2003.

The Colombian government argues that the AUC is not under the command of the armed forces, that they have their own central command structure and should be seen as an autonomous fighting force. This is for the most part true: The AUC's roughly 13,000 armed fighters don't belong to or take orders from the public security forces. What exists in Colombia is a situation where detained paramilitary combatants are seldom prosecuted and very often escape (Human Rights Watch reported that since 1998, at least fifteen alleged paramilitary leaders who had been arrested later "walked past prison guards, soldiers and police to freedom")[16]; direct combat between the army and AUC is practically nonexistent[17]; and most significantly, as stated above, the paramilitaries carry out their actions with the protection and collaboration of the armed forces.

Paramilitaries or Guerrillas: The Greater Obstacle to Peace

The fact remains that the armed forces and the AUC share a common enemy in the FARC and ELN, not to mention the many groups considered by both to be sympathetic to the guerrillas, such as peasant organizations, trade unions, human rights activists, and members of the political left. Undoubtedly, the paramilitary question is perhaps the most complicated issue facing Colombia today, although you wouldn't know it if your main source of information was the *New York Times*, *CNN*, or any of the many U.S. news media outlets that cannot seem to get its reporters off the guerrilla-terrorist-drug trafficking bandwagon. Since the 1980s, through their use of terror, the paramilitary groups and their civilian and state collaborators have been key in lessening the possibilities of a negotiated peace between the government and the guerrillas.[18] It would not be a stretch to argue that the paramilitary question was among the principal stumbling blocks that led to the collapse of peace talks between President Andres Pastrana's government and the FARC in February 2002, although it was rarely mentioned in the dozens of postmortems written about the failed peace process in the U.S. media.

The rebel high command repeatedly argued that the government's failure to rein in the AUC was evidence that they were not negotiating in good faith. In Colombia and the United States, however, most of the attention was being directed at how the FARC failed to make any concrete gestures of its own to demonstrate that it was serious about peace. The government pointed to the demilitarization of five southern municipalities controlled by the FARC as a major concession to the guerrillas, carried out against the will of the armed forces high command, yet yielding little in return. Criticism mounted in the Colombian press, first against the FARC for failing to implement a moratorium on the kidnapping of civilians, for example, and later against Pastrana for not standing up to what was described as guerrilla intransigence. Reports in Colombia were issued about how the FARC was using the demilitarized zone to hold kidnap victims, stockpile weapons, and expand its role in coca cultivation and distribution.

Colombia's middle class, suffering from the effects of the country's worst economic recession in sixty years, was becoming increasingly irate, quick to accuse the FARC for all the country's ills. Colombia's peace commissioner at the time, Camilo Gómez Alzate, felt the heat from a skeptical public. This made it difficult for a reasoned debate to emerge about some of the FARC's own proposals relating to crop substitution as an alternative to aerial fumigations, limits on privatization of state industries, and, most important, for the conditions needed to establish a ceasefire.[19] A case was being made in the media that the FARC was violating all sorts of accords it had committed itself to, although the fact of the matter was that no agreements had been signed up to that point. People were quick to forget that they were negotiating under the conditions of ongoing combat, however unpleasant this was to stomach.

As these events unfolded and the peace process kept stalling, the AUC waged its war throughout the country with almost complete impunity. One of the most egregious examples of this occurred in the lush region of El Naya, where the southern departments of Cauca and Valle meet in the Pacific coast of Colombia. Despite repeated warnings from the community that can be traced back to the last few months of 2000, at least 40 and perhaps even as many as 100 people were massacred by paramilitary gunmen operating with the complicity of the armed forces on April 11 and 12, 2001. According to members of the displaced communities from Upper and Lower Naya, the episode actually began in November 2000 when local paramilitaries tortured and killed four people from the municipalities of Santander de Quilichao, Jamundí, Puerto Tejada, and Buenos Aires. This coincided with repeated harassment and threats carried out by other armed groups, including the FARC and ELN, who accused the local peasants of collaborating with the state when they demanded protection from the paramilitaries. It should be mentioned that the FARC was accused of killing four Indian leaders from Cauca in December 2000.

After a series of other assassinations carried out by the paramilitaries, including three local leaders who were killed "200 meters away from a military roadblock set up in broad daylight," the AUC unit issued a demand to residents that they vacate the region or "face the consequences." This led to the displacement of the indigenous community of Paila and the peasant counties of Timba and Santander.[20] These paramilitary attacks prompted a commission of national and international nongovernmental organizations to visit the region in late November 2000. These organizations called on the government to take special measures to protect the civilian population. Although the government eventually sent its own commission to investigate on January 11, 2001, there were "no visible or effective measures taken after it departed to stem paramilitary violence."[21] The Inter-American Commission on Human Rights of the Organization of American States also issued statements urging the government to take the necessary steps to protect the local authorities and the members of social organizations operating in the area.

The tensions in Naya and the warnings of an impending massacre were raised repeatedly by activist Carlos Rosero, executive director of the Colombian nongovernmental organization Procesos de Comunidades Negras (PCN; Process of Black Communities), when he was visiting the United States on a national speaking tour in February and March of 2001. Despite being one of the most respected Afro-Colombian activists in Colombia, his meetings with congressional aides, interviews with local media, and countless talks to community groups in the United States could not prevent what was about to occur in Naya. Nothing was done to secure the area.

According to eyewitnesses who survived the two-day massacre, it all began about a week earlier, when members of the army's Third Brigade entered the Upper Naya in "pursuit of a group of ELN guerrillas," whom the army alleged to have been seen in the area. When residents told the soldiers that they were not aware of the ELN's presence, they were told by the army to "cooperate with us now, because we're more understanding than our 'cousins,'" referring to the local AUC unit. After hours of pressing, the eyewitnesses said, the army commander warned them that "their cousins" will be back soon, and that "we will not be around to protect you."[22] On April 11 and 12, in the middle of Holy Week, paramilitaries stormed through Naya on a "macabre caravan" of murder and plunder, decapitating and cutting off the limbs of their victims, dragging bodies on their motorcycles, and dumping them into the thick forest, all the while raiding the small bodegas and houses of the peasants living in the area. Throughout the massacre, the murderers were heard shouting accusations at their victims, calling them *guerrilleros* (guerrillas) or *milicianos* (militants). In the end, the government recorded twenty-seven deaths and another twenty people missing and presumed dead. All were either indigenous or of African descent. Later the Public Advocate's office said the AUC had killed 40 people and were responsible for the displacement of another 1,000. Carlos Castaño, meanwhile, took credit for many more, pointing to at least 100 victims and referring to the operation as a "glorious patriotic act against subversion."[23]

The true number of victims may never be known, first, because of the manner in which the perpetrators of the massacre disposed of the body parts, and second, because of the fact that it was carried out during Holy Week, when many people were traveling in and out of the region. As a result, it was difficult to determine who was actually killed from inside and outside of Naya. The forced displacement made it even more difficult to make an accurate count.[24]

The tragedy of Naya occurred despite strong evidence linking the army's Third Brigade with the formation of several paramilitary units in the departments of Cauca and Valle as far back as 1999. According to Human Rights Watch, Colombian government investigators had provided them

> with detailed information showing that in 1999 the Colombian Army's Third Brigade helped set up a paramilitary group, called the Calima Front. Investigators

from the Attorney General's office [said] they had compiled compelling evidence linking the Calima Front to active duty, retired, and reserve military officers attached to the Third Brigade along with local landowners and hired paramilitaries taken from the ranks of AUC. According to these government investigators as well as eyewitness testimony . . . , the Third Brigade provided the Calima Front with weapons, intelligence, and logistical support and coordinated actions with them.[25]

Unfortunately, the Colombian military and the hawks within the government were too preoccupied with discrediting the guerrillas to worry too much about these pesky human rights reports. The people whose interest the paramilitaries were serving by dislocating so many families and clearing the land for future development remained conspicuously silent, as has been the case in just about every massacre the AUC has carried out over the years. And because the Colombian media and their counterparts in the United States were so eager to follow the lead of official sources in both countries while ignoring the urgent calls of community members, activists, and human rights groups, the countless alarm bells about the impending massacre went unheeded. Ten months after the brutal massacre of Naya, talks between the Pastrana government and the FARC collapsed on the grounds that the guerrillas were not serious about peace.

But Talks Were Off to a Bad Start from Day One

The double standard of treatment between the FARC and the AUC was evident from the very opening stages of the peace talks in January 1999 (and continued perversely in 2003 when the Uribe government and the AUC were engaged in demobilization talks). This double standard enabled the government to promote the idea that it was the FARC that was responsible for the eventual collapse of the peace talks. For example, on the first day of talks, the entire country was focused on the small town of San Vicente del Caguán in the heart of the demilitarized zone where the FARC established its headquarters. Hundreds of guerrillas, international dignitaries, journalists, and other observers gathered for the official launching of the first government-guerrilla dialogue in more than eight years. President Pastrana, elected because of his stated commitment to peace with the rebels, arrived with considerable fanfare. But he was stood up by Manuel Marulanda Vélez, the commander in chief of the FARC, who chose to stay away from the circus-like atmosphere because of what the FARC described as considerable security concerns.

Although the FARC had a high-level delegation made up of most of its secretariat present at the inaugural ceremonies, the front pages of all the Colombian newspapers the next day showed a photograph of the president sitting next to an empty chair, his face betraying the look of a dumbfounded groom who has been left standing alone at the altar by his bride on the day of the wedding. This image was duplicated throughout the world, published in the *New York Times* and about a dozen other U.S. daily papers the next day. It was a public relations gaffe by the FARC's commander, a missed photo opportunity that was meant to set the stage for the renewed talks. How could this guerrilla commander do this to the president in front of all these people?

What was lost in the hoopla after Marulanda broke his appointment with the president, however, was the fact that during that same thirty-six-hour period, more than 150 people were killed by paramilitary death squads in different parts of the country, a personal message from the AUC that they were not happy about the highly publicized peace talks with their archenemies.

This loss of life did not make half the splash in the U.S. press, with the *New York Times* picking it up as a world news brief several days later. In the Colombian press, the results were even more extreme. For more than a week, columnists and pundits focused on the terrible message the FARC's commander sent by missing the inaugural ceremony, while hardly mentioning the AUC's highly orchestrated bloodbath. For the next three years, the double standard continued.[26]

In fact, led by its charismatic leader Carlos Castaño, the AUC successfully cultivated an image through favorable coverage in the Colombian media as the legitimate "third actor" in the conflict that warranted the same political recognition granted to the guerrillas. Castaño gave interviews to some of the leading publications in the country where he answered softball questions about the origins of his crusade, allowing him to emerge as a victim of guerrilla terror, describing in detail how his father had been kidnapped and killed by the FARC in the 1980s. Castaño's memoir *My Confession* was one of the most popular books in Colombia, selling in all the major cities and providing the public with a sympathetic portrait of a mass murderer.[27] In this environment, President Pastrana *and* the FARC both lost the public's faith in the legitimacy of the talks, while the AUC gained the political upper hand, especially among Colombia's middle and upper classes.

Meanwhile, militarily, the AUC consolidated its hold on the Middle Magdalena region, and in particular in the southern part of the department of Bolívar. This is where the paramilitaries were challenging the establishment of a so-called coexistence zone that was being set up by the Pastrana government to begin peace talks with the ELN, a process that never got off the ground. Through the use of the kind of terror just described, the AUC also expanded into the departments of North Santander and Chocó, as well as into the Sierra Nevada mountains of Santa

Marta on the Atlantic Coast, experiencing its most rapid growth yet in terms of numbers of combatants. Although these developments could not be entirely ignored by the Colombian media, very few people were making the political connections about their significance. In short, the intensification of the conflict from the AUC's standpoint was a direct reaction to the peace negotiations that had been started by Pastrana in an effort to neutralize (or reverse) any possible changes in the balance of forces that may have resulted from those negotiations.[28] Not surprisingly, the armed forces did little to alter this landscape given their own profound discomfort with the peace process. Colombian philosopher Luis Alberto Restrepo of the National University of Bogotá put it best when he wrote: "So long as the Colombian State sees itself ever more besieged by the guerrillas, no administration will be in the position of wanting or being able to confront paramilitary groups that have now become . . . a veritable irregular army."[29]

Along with the ongoing collaboration between elements of the army and the AUC, today there are approximately 1,000 active AUC members who have served in the Colombian military, including fifty-three retired military officers who have served as advisors to the AUC. They have up to fourteen state-of-the-art helicopters, a dozen small planes, and countless speedboats with mounted machine guns to use in their war against the guerrillas.[30] Indeed, they are a full-fledged army, operating almost with complete impunity throughout the country.

Further complicating matters is the AUC's very lucrative source of funding that includes drug trafficking and money laundering. Indeed, while the FARC is seen to generate considerable financial resources from its links to the bottom end of the drug trade—that is, the peasant farmers, processing labs, and jungle air strips described in the previous chapter—the AUC's historic links with the much more lucrative upper end of the drug trade—the major international cartels and landowners who were behind their creation in the 1980s—has provided them with unbridled economic self-sufficiency. In this regard, it is correct to say that narcotrafficking has been the primary fuel for the latest phase in Colombia's civil war. Between 1997 and 2002, direct confrontations between paramilitaries and guerrillas over the control of some of the primary coca-growing territories in the country led to even further escalation in the war, and of course the displacement of tens of thousands of civilians.

The nature of today's paramilitary forces has changed considerably from the small-scale armed groups they were in the 1980s, when they first emerged within the contemporary context as death squads under the employ of drug traffickers who were tired of paying off guerrillas. The AUC is a national organization, autonomous from the government. They have a clearly defined political agenda that coincides with the agenda of the Colombian political right, and increasingly that of a disgruntled middle class. But they are a far cry from being a "rebel" or "insurgent" army with a fighting force that emerged with a consistent ideology that was designed to confront the established order. Colombian sociologist Fernando Cubides of the National University describes it as "an ideology forged a posteriori, after actions have occurred, in order to justify them." The actions, of course, are the massacres, the gruesome attacks against civilians thought to be guerrilla collaborators. Cubides argues that, as a result of these actions, the general propaganda posture of the AUC leaders reflects "a tone aimed at exonerating themselves and tends to follow the argumentative logic of the defense in a judicial proceeding." This explains their complex evolution from a broad array of "self-defense" and private militias whose raison d'être was protecting private interests, including drug traffickers, to the national umbrella organization that exists today.

Cubides argues that originally the violent actions were committed in a private context, but

> the logic of confrontation places them on a broader stage. The type of enemy against whom they fight envelops them in issues of territorial domination and the questions of disaffected populations. It then becomes indispensable for them to find a cause, make explicit their extra-individual motivations, and add a public end to their private goals. Pursuing efficacy in combat, they replicate the strategic orientation . . . of the guerrillas and imitate their underground network. They learn that they can reap dividends by maintaining ties to legal politics and thus hope to be included in eventual negotiations.[31]

This strategy began to reap concrete political benefits by the summer of 2003. While Uribe was executing his all-out, national military counteroffensive against the guerrillas, his commissioner for peace, Carlos Alberto Restrepo, was involved in secret talks with the top leadership of the AUC. Their goal: dismantling the paramilitary apparatus by 2006. This process was described widely in the Colombian media as "peace negotiations," although many observers were quick to discredit the terminology, opting instead to call them "demobilization" talks. Regardless, it was becoming difficult to avoid noticing that this was a deliberate strategy to rein in the paramilitaries in order to legitimize the state, thus facilitating a major offensive against the real troublemakers, the FARC and ELN.

A New Role for the Paramilitaries

The paramilitary experiment may have outlived its usefulness from the standpoint of the Colombian government. Today, President Uribe's team must present itself before the international community as a true fighter against all kinds of terrorism in order to justify its broader, authoritarian strategy of order and control, and to continue receiving the financial and political support from abroad that it desperately needs. Indeed, Uribe's "Democratic Defense and Security Policy" is aimed at establishing a legitimate state presence in the places where its absence has allowed for the growth of both guerrilla and paramilitary forces. Uribe cannot afford to allow the armed forces to maintain the open links to the AUC that it has maintained for so many years. He has therefore incorporated the paramilitaries into the antiterrorism rhetoric that has become so popular within Colombia and the rest of the world.

This "change" in approach is especially important for Uribe because of the negative image he came in with as being the "paramilitary president," an assessment based on his performance as governor of Antióquia in the early 1990s, where he was responsible for establishing armed militias known as the *Convivir—Asociaciones Comunitarias de Seguridad,* or Community Security Associations. The *Convivir* were criticized by human rights groups, including Amnesty International, as being a violation of international humanitarian law because they made civilians both potential victims and victimizers in the military conflict.[32] The *Convivir* model is the basis of Uribe's current strategy of creating a one-million-person "civilian patrol" to assist the armed forces in its "counterterrorism" war throughout the country, what some observers described as the legitimization of the paramilitary experiment.[33] The so-called *Convivir* were authorized by the minister of defense and enjoyed a rapid boom that eventually spread beyond Medellín. Yet they did not vanish from the landscape once they were outlawed in 1999. According to various sources, the rank and file of the *Convivir* made themselves readily available to the paramilitaries and, in fact, were instrumental in the accelerated growth the AUC experienced in the late 1990s.

Another important factor in the shift in tactics was the need for the Colombian military to demonstrate to the world that it was indeed capable of defeating or at least hitting the guerrillas very hard on the battlefield, something it had not been able to do consistently in almost four decades of fighting. Some observers argue that, precisely because of the military's own failures, the AUC has gained so much respect and support in recent years: It was able to make substantial gains in terms of pushing the FARC and ELN out of certain territories, especially in Urabá and in parts of southern Colombia. This was done specifically by creating terror and fear in what was considered the FARC's civilian "support" base and not necessarily by direct combat with the guerrillas. As a result of the forced displacement caused by this terror, the paramilitaries were able to take control of some of these areas with the collaboration of the army.

For too long, the armed forces were seen as an incompetent, corrupt, and militarily inept institution that needed a major overhaul in order to win the war against the guerrillas. The way to turn this around was through more extensive training from the United States. There was an urgent need to professionalize the armed forces, make it more mobile and more able to adapt to the hit and run tactics of the guerrillas. Of course, this could be accomplished only through more military spending. The military budget increased from 1.8 percent of the gross domestic product in 1994 to 3.7 percent by 2000. President Uribe has already called for even more money for the military budget, aided by the now famous Uribe war tax (and of course by the United States). With this renewed investment in the legitimate military, the government had to show results quickly, both to Colombians and to the rest of the world. Part of these results included the neutralization of the guerrillas on the battlefield, but just as important was the rupture once and for all of the AUC–armed forces alliance and the dismantling of the paramilitaries.

On a political level, this did not seem to pose too many problems for the AUC and its backers—large landowners, traditional agribusiness people, cattle ranchers, and yes, drug traffickers. As Carlos Castaño stated on several occasions in media interviews since August 2002, they have come to realize that under Uribe's watch, the extreme right has nothing to worry about in terms of losing influence or power within Colombia. Indeed, their wishes will most likely be respected, the most fundamental being the destruction of the guerrillas. Furthermore, at least 35 percent of the Colombian Congress is said to be controlled by lawmakers considered to be AUC supporters.[34] With Uribe promoting sweeping constitutional and other political reforms to give more power to the executive, more liberties to the state security forces, and the broader consolidation of the neoliberal economic program, the AUC can finally rest easy, knowing that their will has won out within "legitimate" mechanisms.

Undoubtedly, the major factor influencing the paramilitary's willingness to shift its strategy from the military to the political front, however, was the federal indictment handed down in September 2002 by the U.S. Justice Department against the top AUC leadership, including Carlos Castaño. The indictment and extradition request charged Castaño and two other AUC members—military commander Salvatore Mancuso, and Juan Carlos Sierra Ramírez—with five counts of drug trafficking, with each facing sentences of up to life imprisonment if convicted of all charges. U.S. Drug Enforcement Agency (DEA) administrator Asa Hutchinson said it was "clear that the paramilitary organization led by Carlos Castaño was immersed for years in the illegal drug trade, from the taxing of coca growers to the processing laboratories to the transportation of cocaine to the targeted country."

Attorney General John Ashcroft talked about the "interdependence between terrorists that threaten American lives and the illegal drugs that threaten America's potential."[35] How Castaño's terrorism affected Colombian lives or potential, quite often with the direct support of Washington's allies in the Colombian armed forces, was not Ashcroft's main concern. Nevertheless, there is no question that the indictment, and the polemic the extradition request created within the paramilitary organization, had a direct impact on the AUC's decision to announce a ceasefire at the end of 2002, opening the way for initial talks with representatives of Uribe's government. With Uribe so dependent on U.S. military assistance, he was not going to take the indictment lightly. Castaño clearly understood this and, fearing the possibility of extradition to the United States, decided it was time to find a way out of his status of "illegality."[36]

An Uribe-appointed exploratory commission began to hold secret meetings with the AUC in January 2003, the paramilitary leadership well aware that they would be treated quite differently than the FARC or the ELN. Just in the language used to describe the talks, one immediately got a sense of how certain "terrorist groups" would be handled with considerably different criteria within the contemporary Colombian context. On January 7, 2003, President Uribe said, "All [peace] processes which remove factors of violence from the country are useful for the tranquility of Colombians and will lighten the human rights situation."[37] It was a far cry from the language he reserved for the FARC and the ELN.

On July 15, 2003, in the town of Santa Fe de Ralito in the heart of Córdoba, paramilitary country, members of the government's exploratory commission led by Luis Carlos Restrepo met with Castaño, Mancuso, and seven other leaders of the AUC under a banner that read "AUC-Gobierno, una esperanza de paz," ("AUC-Government, a hope for peace"). Together with observers from the Catholic Church, the two sides officially announced the start of formal negotiations that would eventually lead to the demobilization of 13,000 AUC fighters by December 31, 2005, and their gradual reincorporation into civilian life. After seven months of silence during secret talks, the announcement was greeted with universal enthusiasm by the Colombian media. Commentators wrote how President Uribe, who came into office with a pledge to dismantle "los violentos," was already beginning to make good on his promise to re-establish the state's legitimacy, at least on one front. This provided the president with even more favorable news coverage.

The AUC, meanwhile, was presented in newspapers, magazines, and television as a reasonable organization that, unlike the FARC in its peace talks with Pastrana, was willing to disarm and work constructively to end the years of violence it had carried out in the countryside. News reports were quick to point out that the AUC did not demand a "demilitarized zone" as a condition to the talks, and they commended the AUC for sticking to its unilateral ceasefire made at the end of 2002. That the AUC did *not* demand the defeat of the guerrillas as a precondition to talks was also presented as evidence of the paramilitary's reasonable approach to the government, in stark contrast to the FARC.[38] Mancuso and Castaño granted extensive interviews to the major national television networks, expressing remorse for all the years of conflict while repeatedly stating that "their time had come and gone" as an illegal organization. Clearly they were making use of the public relations gains made in the previous years.

In fact, they used this powerful national platform to promote the legal document made public a few weeks earlier by the weekly news magazine *Cambio*, whereby the AUC made its legal case for reincorporation into civilian life. The mantra that was beginning to emerge was: "If trying to topple the constitutional regime is considered a political crime, then so is it to go up in arms to defend that regime, which is the specific, concrete and unquestionable case of the self-defense groups."[39] More than fifteen years of massacres, assassinations, disappearances, and forced displacements were being made to look as "the product of an irregular war, aimed at combating, and at containing subversion and its auxiliaries."[40]

Needless to say, a lot of major obstacles remain and are sure to be the focus of intense internal debates within Colombia throughout the remainder of Uribe's term, which expires in 2006. One major issue is which groups within the larger paramilitary infrastructure are to be included in the demobilization process? While Castaño is said to be in command of 13,000 combatants, the government estimates another 6,500 to 7,000 paramilitaries are not involved in the current dialogue, most of whom refuse to demobilize while the guerrillas continue fighting. Some analysts argue that this reflects the deep divisions within the ranks of the paramilitaries, an indication that, to a certain extent, the situation got out of Castaño's control. Among those not covered in the preliminary talks, for example, are the powerful *Bloque Central Bolívar* and the *Alianza Oriente de los Llanos*, both involved in separate talks, as well as the *Bloque del Magdalena Medio*. Add to this the numerous urban militias tied to the paramilitaries that have been waging war in some of the poorest sections of Medellín, Bogotá, and other big cities, and it becomes clear from the outset that the paramilitary apparatus will not be so easily dismantled.

Tied to the issue of demobilization are the questions of who is going to pay for it, how will the process be monitored, and will there be guarantees of protection for the soon-to-be former AUC combatants? The cost of demobilizing the AUC is estimated to be $16,000 per person for the first two years alone, totaling about $208 million. The government simply does not have the means to pay for this. Although both the European Union and the United States have indicated a willingness to help cover some of the tab, it is still a far cry from the overall costs that such a process requires.[41] Furthermore, even if the resources were found to successfully reincorporate them into civilian life, what kind of protections will be provided to prevent actions of retribution against them, and what guarantees will exist to make sure they don't pick up arms again? President Uribe has proposed bringing in United Nations peacekeepers to the areas where the AUC will concentrate and demobilize, a suggestion that raised considerable protests from many sectors within Colombia, not the least of which being the guerrillas. As 2003 was coming to a close, none of these issues was anywhere near to being resolved.

The Most Significant Concern About the Process: Impunity

The hundreds of thousands of victims of paramilitary terror continue to argue that "national reconciliation" cannot take place behind the closed doors of government-AUC talks while justice takes a back seat to some kind of paramilitary amnesty.[42] For years the issue of whether or not the government should hold a dialogue with the AUC has been among the most contentious points of debate, especially among Colombian progressives. Many human rights activists and opposition politicians argue that the process underway with the AUC should not be described as a peace negotiation because that would require a dialogue between two opposing forces, or enemies. Considering the historical links between the state and the paramilitaries, the objection makes sense. It should be more accurately described as the government putting its own house in order in an attempt to gain legitimacy for its military and police forces. This is the premise of Uribe's Democratic Defense and Security Policy. Ironically, this has been one of the principal demands of the FARC all along: control the "paras," and we'll talk in good faith. Of course, Uribe has no intention of talking to the guerrillas, at least not until they are ready for unconditional surrender.

Because of the military, economic, and political weight that the AUC has accumulated over the last ten years, however, the government had no choice but to sit down and make deals with its command structure in order to incorporate them into a post-war Colombia. In fact, there are historical precedents for such talks with the so-called *autodefensas* in the 1960s and even as recently as the early 1990s. Today, the justification for such talks relies on the pragmatic argument that the AUC has evolved into a third force in the conflict that, in many ways, has tilted the balance of power. People supporting talks insist that some kind of legal arrangement must be made between the AUC and the government if there is to be any kind of long-term peace agreement reached in the country.

The key question is, At what cost should these talks take place in terms of justice to the victims of paramilitary terror? Is the demobilization process another way of certifying impunity for the thousands of crimes against humanity carried out by AUC combatants? Will there be reparations for the millions of internally displaced people, many of whom lost family members due to the relentless violence? Will the people and institutions, both public and private, who have backed the paramilitaries be permanently exposed and held accountable, or will they escape from the process unscathed?

Judging from the government's initial statements on the issue, they are considering several possibilities based on Colombian criminal law. For example, those low-level combatants who agree to turn in their weapons and commit themselves to civilian life will be covered in a general amnesty that is provided for in crimes of sedition under Colombian law. As for those combatants who clearly have charges pending against them for crimes against humanity committed in their campaign of terror on the civilian population, they will be prosecuted under the law, go through some kind of legal proceeding, and, if convicted, will be sentenced and punished for these crimes. In defending this process, Peace Commissioner Luis Carlos Restrepo said in all cases the truth will not be compromised. The interesting point in this instance, however, is that the government is considering alternatives to incarceration for the convicted terrorists, such as community service functions, building new homes for victims of the violence, and turning over land stolen from civilians. Needless to say, there is nothing close to a universal consensus on the issue, and human rights groups have expressed grave concerns. What's important to point out is that the emphasis placed by the government on this level of justice makes it appear as if the problem of paramilitarism in Colombia was simply one of armed peasants who were either voluntarily or forcibly recruited to carry out a war against the guerrillas, and now it was simply time to bring these misguided boys home, so to speak. The systematic nature of the dirty war is thereby swept under the rug, the latest installment in Colombia's archive of forgotten history.

Which brings us to the most troubling aspects of the so-called demobilization process of the AUC. First, what is going to happen to its top leadership, including Castaño and Mancuso? Although the State Department welcomed the process underway between the government and the AUC, Phil Chicola, Under-Secretary of State for Andean Affairs, said clearly Washington would not abandon the extradition requests. The extradition issue was not discussed in the initial talks between government officials and the paramilitary leadership, although both Castaño and Mancuso on several occasions expressed their unwillingness to face justice in U.S. courts. Mancuso told *El Tiempo*, for example: "I am willing to talk with them [the United States] about the extradition whenever they want. As soon as it becomes clear to them who we really are and where we are going, the sooner they will realize what role they should play in a peaceful solution to the armed conflict in Colombia."[43] This kind of language immediately raised concerns that there is a distinct possibility Uribe might try to negotiate with the United States to get Castaño and Mancuso off Washington's extradition request list in the interest of "peace and stability." It also raised the possibility of having these war criminals face charges in another country, much like the cases against Chilean dictator Augusto Pinochet and the Argentine military junta initiated by Spanish judge Baltasar Garzón.

Second, and perhaps more important, what will happen to the dozens of military personnel, both retired and active, police officials, local and national authorities, prosecutors, industrialists, landowners, cattle ranchers, businessmen, and narcotraffickers who for years have been financing and/or collaborating directly with the paramilitary forces? Will these individuals receive get-out-of-jail-free cards, or will they be held accountable for their direct responsibility in the dirty war? If one were dependent solely on official sources for information, one would get the impression that these individuals do not even exist. The Colombian news media focused a considerable amount of attention on the reasonable concern expressed by government prosecutors that some big-time drug lords may try to take advantage of the political process with the paramilitaries in order to wash their hands of drug-trafficking charges. Not surprisingly, however, these same media sources paid less attention to the close links the AUC has maintained with so-called legitimate actors in both the public and private sectors, links that allowed the terrorist organization to flourish and expand over the past fifteen years, and that from the looks of things would remain unchanged as part of the demobilization process.[44]

At the risk of being written off as an alarmist, what has

become apparent to me is that the AUC's mission of repression, control, and violence will not be going away any time soon, even if they do reach a long-term "accord" with Uribe. If anything, by most accounts it appears that the paramilitary experiment is becoming institutionalized under the guise of the government's democratic security strategy of consolidation and control.

During his first year in office, concerns mounted about Uribe's large network of civilian informers designed to help the army in its war against "terrorism." The system is completely reminiscent of the *Convivir* civilian militias that were started by Uribe in Medellín but were eventually made illegal in the late 1990s. The government's argument in defense of this network of informants is that regular Colombian citizens must collaborate with the state, that the public must play a role in defeating terrorism by confiding in and collaborating with legitimate authorities. Under different circumstances perhaps this could be possible, but in a society as polarized as Colombia it may be wishful thinking. Human rights groups have argued this is extremely dangerous for the civilian population because it gets them directly involved in the armed conflict. Furthermore, this system of "citizen informants" may ultimately prove to be unreliable because of the strong possibility that deliberate misinformation will be provided to authorities as a way to settle old scores with real and potential enemies. This is no way to promote citizen participation.

With considerable fanfare, the government also set up so-called peasant armies in the countryside. These peasant armies are legitimate, state-sponsored auxiliaries for the armed forces designed to protect rural communities from "terrorist" incursions. The part-time soldiers would live within their communities at night and serve as a sort of "auxiliary" army by day, helping the regulars confront the guerrillas. Recruitment started in places like Antióquia, Arauca, Chocó, and Cauca in late 2002 with the incentives of a government salary and uniforms. It was universally cheered as yet another example of Uribe's comprehensive approach in confronting the growing terrorist threat. According to some local elected officials and community leaders interviewed in the department of Cauca, a good percentage of the people signing up for these peasant armies are former and active members of the AUC.[45] In essence, it appears as if the many soon-to-be-decommissioned and -unemployed paramilitaries will remain busy once their leaders sign "peace pacts" with the government, something that clearly they are more than qualified to do given their previous on-the-job training. The potential for mass-scale retribution against alleged and actual guerrillas is enormous. Further complicating matters, even if the ranks of the "peasant armies" were filled with individuals who have completely clean records and good intentions, their limited training and part-time status opens them up to a brand new wave of attacks from guerrillas seeking them out as collaborators with the state.

All of this is a dangerous scenario for the future of Colombia, and it is the perfect recipe for further polarization as well as deeper authoritarianism. After one year in office, President Uribe was being widely commended for having developed a strategy that, for once, was providing Colombians a sense of security. The paramilitaries were being "dismantled," while the guerrillas appeared to be on the defensive. But as I pointed out earlier, the guerrillas have demonstrated an extraordinary resilience in responding to increased government militarization and repression in the past. The impunity with which the paramilitaries were being rewarded clearly would not resolve the problems of violence in the countryside, and both the FARC and the ELN would certainly let it be known, notwithstanding their position of apparent weakness in the new environment. It's a cycle of brewing violence that will most likely lead to more war—large scale, rural *and* urban, expansive, all occurring with an increasingly interventionist administration watching closely from the White House. The director of operations for U.S. Southern Command, Brigadier General Galen Jackman, echoed the Bush administration's line in December 2002 when he said, "Our main objective is to help transform the Colombian military to a force that is capable of defeating the terrorist organizations, establishing presence and defense, in order to provide a safe and secure environment and governance throughout Colombia." He added that Colombia has recently crafted a "well thought out, systematic way" for reestablishing governmental authority throughout the country.[46] Apparently, General Jackman has been reading too many of the optimistic and uncritical reports from the Colombian news media while paying little attention to Colombia's tragic history.

Democratic Security or Continued Conflict?

In closing, the counterinsurgency war of the last forty years has been characterized by violence carried out directly by the state's own security forces, and turned over gradually to their paramilitary allies backed by the tremendous resources of the cocaine trade. This horrendous track record of massacres and displacement has been written about in countless human rights reports, academic journals, and news articles. In Colombia, the names have become synonymous with terror: El Nilo, Mapiripán, Santo Domingo, el Naya, Urabá . . . the list could go on and on.

Today, a newly constituted force is slowly emerging whereby legitimate state actors are meant to be the primary protagonists. The dirty war infrastructure of the paramilitaries is being dismantled with the blessing of its top leadership because, as they see it, today "there is a government and there are institutions capable of assuming their responsibilities."[47] This is happening with the primary goal of fighting guerrilla terror and ending the forty-year internal conflict with a military victory. By 2003, polls showed a good percentage of people began to embrace this approach as the solution to the country's problems.

What these polls do not demonstrate is how the culture of fear that was created by the dirty war continues throughout the countryside, and the source of the fear is not solely the guerrillas. In a recent visit to San José, the capital of Guaviare, I spoke to a number of independent political activists who described in great detail the kinds of threats they continued to receive from the paramilitaries that controlled the town, notwithstanding demobilization talks with the government. One member of the San José city council was told directly that he would be better off not running for the departmental assembly in the October 2003 elections unless he registered as a Liberal or Conservative. He refused to cave in to the threats, but as a result was forced to leave the region for several months. Now he is back, well aware that his challenge to the paramilitary authorities may cost him his life. This scenario is played out in every region of the country, democratic security or not!

As I see it, the end result will most likely be more of the same: the silencing of legal sociopolitical resistance, the destruction of community organizations, and the continued displacement of thousands of people from their lands. There is little reason to believe that by expanding its military capacity and implementing more draconian security measures, all with the increased support from the United States, the government of Uribe will fundamentally transform this reality. There is an urgent need to address the issues described earlier that have led to the political, economic, and sociocultural marginalization and exclusion of the vast majority of the Colombian people.

Clearly, the guerrillas must bear much of the responsibility for the rapid deterioration of the civil conflict and the failure of the most recent round of peace talks in 2002. Their attacks against the country's infrastructure does nothing to promote social and economic justice for the people they supposedly are there to defend. Their national and indeed international isolation is in many ways of their own doing. But does this mean we should accept the simplistic arguments of the Uribe administration that present the guerrillas as senseless criminals and drug-trafficking terrorists, all the while embracing an ongoing dialogue with the AUC? I would think not. To do so is to negate the political and social roots of the insurgency. Worse yet, it is to ignore the years of dirty war tactics employed by the Colombian state to confront not only the armed opposition, but those sectors of society that through constitutionally protected means have challenged the hegemony of the Colombian elite and its very undemocratic political power structure. Today these observations are rarely made in Colombia; when they are made, they are written off as irrelevant, either by Colombian officials or by conservative pundits, all of whom have taken advantage of the global antiterrorism crusade to fit it squarely into the Colombian context.

As I will try to demonstrate in part 3, the view of Colombia from the United States is not much different. The negation of history almost becomes a prerequisite to shaping policy, a policy ostensibly designed to combat drug trafficking, fortify the Colombian state in order to strengthen democracy, and protect U.S. national security interests. For decades, U.S. policy has not been successful in achieving any of these goals, perhaps with the exception of the last one, depending on how one defines U.S. "interests." Nevertheless, the remedies remain more or less the same. Is this a coincidence, or just simply bad luck? In order to try to answer this question, it pays to look at some of the characteristics of U.S. economic and military policies and the way they have evolved over the years. It is also instructive to see how U.S. media quite often reflect policymakers' tendency to overlook historical precedent in contemporary news accounts about the conflict in Colombia. Given the track record of repeated failures, the negligence becomes almost tragic.

III

A View from the North

5

National Security, Dependency, and Exploitation: Bogotá and Washington's Complicit Dance

The role of the United States in Colombia is the subject of considerable debate and discussion within Colombian political and intellectual circles, throughout the nongovernmental organization (NGO) community and the news media, and of course among the general population, cutting across class lines. In many respects the close connections between the two countries have led to a love-hate relationship that Colombian society has developed with its powerful northern neighbor. This relationship is reflected in the general concerns that all Colombians share about national sovereignty and the deep-rooted suspicions that exist as a result of the long history of U.S. interventions in the region. At the same time, there is a widespread admiration for and an embrace of the United States, its people, and its culture, especially among the country's middle class (notwithstanding the reluctance of most people to acknowledge such feelings).

Moving beyond such cultural nuances, however, it is safe to argue that there is a tendency on the part of Colombian intellectuals to be very critical of the role Washington has played in Colombia's internal conflict, with some placing considerable blame squarely on U.S. policymakers for the situation in which the country currently finds itself. Antonio Cabellero, one of the most controversial and respected Colombian columnists, wrote recently: "In the origin of the last fifty years of catastrophe that we have suffered can be found two categorical strategic decisions attributable directly to the governments of the United States." The first decision, made during the period of *La Violencia*, was to place all of the social issues in Latin America squarely "into the framework of the global anti-Communist crusade," resulting in a doctrine that "maintained and reinforced political, economic and military power in the hands of the most reactionary elements of the society." The second decision was made about thirty years later and placed Colombia in the center of even further militarization and conflict: "The declaration of the universal war on drugs . . . a war that was declared abroad, but fought almost exclusively here [in Colombia]."[1]

Although this analysis comes dangerously close to oversimplifying Colombia's national crisis into a knee-jerk, "blame the empire" modality, recent events demonstrate that policies developed in Washington have directly impacted Colombia's internal political, economic, and security situation in an adverse way. Naturally, as Caballero accurately points out, Colombian public officials and the country's economic elite must bear much of the responsibility for the way these policies have been implemented internally. As has already been pointed out, this has often been done with their own interests in mind at the expense of the interests of the rest of the population, all the while facilitating a general surrender of the national sovereignty.

It also needs to be pointed out that U.S. policy is not shaped solely by a homogeneous collective of bureaucrats that agree on the prescriptions needed to resolve the myriad problems facing Colombia. Indeed, in criticizing the dictates of past and present U.S. administrations, there is a tendency to overlook the differences of opinion that actually exist within the U.S. Congress, the

State Department, the Pentagon, and the White House over issues of human rights, military assistance, economic development, and counterdrug strategies. Anybody working closely on Colombia policy in Washington would attest to this reality.

Nevertheless, there is considerable evidence that the general thrust of U.S. policy vis-à-vis Colombia over the years has remained consistent. As I mentioned in the Introduction, for years the United States concerned itself with fighting the war on drugs, investing millions of dollars on a primarily military approach. This has led to a further escalation in the internal military conflict, an increasingly deteriorating human rights crisis, and a general failure to put a dent in the international drug trade. In the end, only a tiny fraction of both the Colombian and U.S. populations has been well served by these policies. Since September 11, 2001, the drug war has been put on the back burner in favor of the more pressing issue of counterterrorism. This has been the justification for even further U.S. involvement, with the long-term impact still unknown. Tragically, as a result, the possibilities for a fundamental transformation of these policies have diminished considerably.

You Scratch My Back, I'll Scratch Yours

Colombia's dependence on Washington for military and economic support stretches far back, a dependency that has dictated Colombian domestic security policy since the 1950s. At the time, U.S. military and intelligence services made their first bilateral agreements with Colombia in the interest of hemispheric defense and in response to the ongoing presence of peasant guerrilla organizations that were fighting the government. This is the period when, according to Caballero, Washington made its first major "decision" regarding how to deal with Colombia and the region as a whole: The communist threat had to be confronted in every corner of the globe, especially in "our own backyard."

Colombian involvement in international conflicts such as the Korean War was directly tied to its dependency on the United States. Colombia was the only country in all of Latin America to respond positively to Washington's call for a direct military role in Korea. Historian David Bushnell writes that Colombia's participation in the Korean War, which involved one battalion of army troops at any given time and the use of a Colombian naval vessel off Korean waters, was primarily a way for then-president Laureano Gomez "to erase any lingering bad impressions caused among U.S. policymakers by his previous attitude [of anti-U.S. sentiment in World War II], and thereby assure himself of a continued flow of U.S. economic and military aid."[2] Pressure from Washington continued on many different levels through the 1960s, 1970s, and 1980s. The civilian leadership in Colombia, always under pressure from the military hierarchy, readily acquiesced as a sure-fire way to guarantee continued assistance, whether or not it was in the best interests of Colombia itself.

The second major "decision" made by Washington that has directly impacted Colombia was to embark on the "global war against narcotrafficking"; although the drug war was launched more than twenty-five years ago, one could safely argue that the latest phase of this war was declared by former president George Bush in 1989. In his inaugural address, the first President Bush referred to drug trafficking as a "clear and present danger" threatening the national security of the United States. This was of course the early days of the post–Cold War, and the United States was searching for a new sense of purpose in order to maintain its powerful military and security infrastructure intact and make people quickly forget about the potential for a "peace dividend." In September of that year, as the drug war was being launched, Bush's chief of staff, John Sununu, went so far as to say that the president would send troops into Colombia, if asked by his Colombian counterpart, Virgilio Barco, because Americans thought the drug problem was so important they'd be willing "to take that risk."[3] The drug war had become Bush's raison d'être, and the militarization of that war was the approach, notwithstanding reservations from Colombians that this was not necessarily what they needed to combat the problem. For example, although 85 to 90 percent of antinarcotics operations in Colombia at the time were being conducted by the Colombian national police, about 85 percent of the $65 million in emergency U.S. aid was being spent on equipment for the army and the air force, sectors of the Colombian government that had been implicated in substantial human rights abuses.[4]

At around the same time, the U.S. government's insistence on extraditing the top leaders of the Medellín cartel to face drug-trafficking charges in the United States created a major controversy within Colombia. Many people saw it as a direct affront to Colombian sovereignty. Others felt it was the only way to bring these criminals to justice. The Colombian government was handcuffed due to the political pressure being applied from the United States. The end result was a wave of violent terrorist attacks carried out by the drug mafias resulting in the deaths of hundreds of Colombians. So much for U.S. policies designed to help Colombia. For the next ten years, when it came to Colombia, the drug war remained the top priority of several administrations, both Democrat and Republican, with very little results to show for their efforts.

In the recent context, one of the most obviously opportunistic examples of Colombian officials currying favor with the White House occurred during the initial stages of the United Nations' weapons inspections in Iraq in December 2002. The rotating president of the UN Security Council, Colombia's ambassador to the United Nations, Alfonso Valdivieso, facilitated the turnover of thousands of Iraqi documents about its weapons programs to the United States before the Security Council could get a hold of them, a clear disregard of diplomatic protocol. The argument presented publicly was that the copying facilities at the State Department were much more efficient than those at the UN headquarters. Yet it was very clear that Valdivieso's quarterback sneak was a nice way to secure even further military assistance for the Colombian government in its expanding war against its own brand of domestic "terrorists."

Not surprisingly, Colombia was the only South American country to openly support the U.S. military attack on Baghdad (Panama, Nicaragua, Costa Rica, Honduras, and El Salvador were the only other regional members of the "coalition"). This controversial decision by President Uribe paid off with the announcement in late March 2003 of an additional $105 million in "counterterrorism" aid that the Bush administration pushed through just as the bombing of Iraq began. The generous gift from Washington padded the already hefty $500 million in aid destined to Colombia for fiscal year 2004. One State Department official was quoted in *El Tiempo* as saying, "There's no doubt that Uribe's backing [of the war on Iraq] demonstrates that he is a friend, that we speak the same language, and that we face the same threats."[5] Meanwhile, opposition members of Colombia's Congress expressed their outrage with this affront to Colombian national sovereignty. One independent legislator, in a dramatic session on the floor of the chamber of representatives, presented Uribe and his ministers a pair of knee pads with American flags painted on them in a symbolic gesture that needed no translation. Most Colombians opposed the war in Iraq and saw Uribe's support clearly for what it was: an opportunistic way to remain in the good graces of the Bush administration.

Whether it's called mutual dependency or superpower coercion, it is not always as obvious as the above-mentioned examples. Going a bit further back in recent history, one has to look a little more carefully to see how military dependency on the United States has had a profound impact on Colombia's internal policies. The malleability of Colombian leaders became readily apparent in 1998 when the Conservative Party leader Andres Pastrana became president and the $1.3 billion *Plan Colombia* aid package materialized. Prior to his election, Pastrana talked about the need to resolve the thirty-four-year civil conflict as a first step to addressing the drug problem in Colombia. In campaign speeches, he argued that only after a comprehensive peace was signed with the guerrillas would the social conditions exist to adequately tackle the root causes of the illicit drug trade, which is poverty and a lack of economic development in many areas of the country where coca and poppy is grown, areas that happen to be under the control of the guerrillas.

Plan Colombia initially was a development strategy for the areas most affected by the conflict and most marginalized in terms of basic human necessities. Modeled after the post-World War II Marshall Plan that rebuilt Europe, it addressed the many conditions behind the drug trade and the internal armed conflict, such as economic inequality, lack of opportunities for progress, especially for Colombian youth, and an unequal distribution of land. It also addressed questions relating to the collapse and general lack of institutional legitimacy and the minimal capacity to govern on the part of local and national authorities. It raised issues such as respect for human rights and the creation of truly participatory democracy as necessary steps in eradicating the fundamental seeds of the conflict. Even among traditional critics of Colombian state policies, such as members of NGOs, human rights activists, and sectors of the different social movements, there was some room for optimism with Pastrana's approach to the problem.

After Pastrana's first visit to Washington, however, he made a sudden about-face. As one Colombian observer put it, Washington's response was that *Plan Colombia* was but a "catalog of good intentions" that needed considerable editing.[6] Pastrana's new line was that the drug issue needed to be resolved first if peace were to come to Colombia, and the only way to do this was to step up U.S. military aid. The earlier language that focused on the needs of the countryside and the profound poverty that fueled the conflict was thoroughly altered. His proposed $7 billion reconstruction program emerged with a commitment from Washington to the tune of $1.3 billion in aid, more than 70 percent of which would be directed toward military and security measures designed to fight the "drug war." *Plan Colombia* was presented to the world as a Colombian initiative. Thus, the arrogant, almost ethnocentric determination that the only solutions to resolve these problems must emanate from Washington in the name of U.S. national security is disguised as a bilateral approach designed by like-minded people in both countries. Policy decisions promoted by the United States a decade earlier that had exacerbated the social and economic conditions for many Colombians were conveniently swept aside and forgotten. And with few exceptions, other factors driving the policy such as U.S. economic interests in Colombia remained hidden, perhaps because they were not as easily justifiable in the eyes of public opinion.

The Seeds of Discontent Were Planted by the United States Years Before *Plan Colombia*

Talk to anybody working in independent social organizations and they'll point to the neoliberal economic program implemented over the last fifteen years as one of the primary catalysts behind the rapid deterioration of the conflict, a fact not fully addressed by *Plan Colombia*'s primarily military thrust. President Cesar Gaviria's decision to resolve Colombia's debt crisis through the route of the major multinational financial institutions set in motion a number of developments that led to the social and economic crisis that we are witnessing today.

Gaviria's so-called *apertura economica*, or economic opening—a step taken in order to fall into the good graces of the United States, the major banks up north, and other international investors—practically marked the end for Colombia's agricultural sector. As a result, by 2001, 80.5 percent of people in the countryside were living below the poverty level, up from 65 percent in 1993. More than 33 percent of the rural population was living in extreme poverty.[7] The devastating impact of Gaviria's policies was felt everywhere, but perhaps it was felt most clearly in the coffee sector, once seen as the pride of Colombia's exports. The *apertura* was followed by the gutting of a worldwide agreement that had held coffee prices stable, benefiting Colombia's small family coffee farms. Since then, global production has outstripped demand and sent prices tumbling, especially for the high-quality beans produced in Colombia. Almost immediately these developments led to a flood of cheap coffee entering Colombia from Vietnam, Brazil, and other countries. This, combined with lessening worldwide demand for Colombia's high-grade beans, sent many local farmers into bankruptcy and pushed unemployment above 20 percent in the coffee-growing region, making it easier for guerrillas and paramilitary forces to gain ground and recruit the rising number of unemployed youth. It also caused many farmers to abandon coffee altogether, choosing instead to plant coca.[8]

If the collapse of the coffee trade could be attributed to other factors beyond the control of Colombian and U.S. policymakers, the responsibility for other negative developments in the agricultural sector lies right at the doorsteps of both Bogotá and Washington. To many people, the economic opening represented the fundamental contradiction in U.S. counterdrug policy. On the one hand peasant farmers were being overwhelmed by the sudden influx of cheaper imported agricultural products, while on the other hand they were losing state subsidies and credits for their own crops. Credits were primarily made available to larger farming associations and organizations, yet at astronomically high interest rates. Smaller, independent peasant farmers had no way to compete, especially in the poorest rural areas lacking infrastructure or any other type of mechanism to get their "legitimate" products to market. This had always been a problem, but it was exacerbated by the neoliberal reforms pushed from Washington.

Survival instincts gave many small and mid-size farmers only one alternative: cultivate coca. In 1995, when I asked one coca farmer from the southern municipality of Miraflores in the department of Guaviare why she was growing coca, she responded quite simply: "If I wanted to sell yucca in the market in San Jose [the capital of the department] it would cost me $2.50 per pound just to get it there. Once there, I could only sell it for $1.00 per pound. You do the math. Does it make any sense to grow yucca? Whereas I grow some coca, the traders come to me to buy the raw materials, they do what they want with it, and I have money to buy shoes for my children." This logic has spread like wildfire throughout southern Colombia, exacerbating the war by making poor peasant farmers the targets of expansive military operations.

The response from the Colombian government, with the blessing from the United States, both before and after *Plan Colombia*, has been to fumigate those "illegitimate" crops and demand that the farmers start growing something else, without providing them substantial assistance or incentives to develop true alternatives. The response from groups like the National Association of Peasant Users (ANUC), has been to resist these policies wholeheartedly, blocking major thoroughfares in massive national and regional mobilizations against the fumigations, and demanding a shift in national priorities to provide credits and assistance to small farmers. In Cauca, indigenous farmers signed several agreements with the government in the mid-1990s, agreeing to manually eradicate coca and poppy cultivations in exchange for development assistance. The government of Ernesto Samper failed to fulfill its pledges of support to the communities, leading to massive protests throughout the department. In Putumayo, "social pacts" signed between the government and coca farmers were supposed to guarantee protection of individual plots, but, according to human rights groups, they did not prevent stepped-up aerial fumigations from destroying legitimate crops. It has been a consistent pattern of promises made and commitments broken, with poor farmers always losing out.

Eventually these farmers found an important ally in Floro Tunubalá, a Guambiano Indian from Cauca who was remarkably elected governor of the department in 2001 behind a major coalition of indigenous, Afro-Colombian, peasant, and independent community organizations. Tunubalá made several visits to Washington with the governors of five other southern departments to demand an end to the aerial fumigation campaign, at least until environmental impact studies could be finalized and economic alternatives could be implemented. In lobbying the Colombian and U.S. governments directly, the governors thought they were practicing democracy, given the widespread opposition to the fumigations in their respective departments. They soon learned the hard way how difficult it is to openly confront the weight of the U.S. government. Ultimately, these actions did not reverse the U.S. fumigation policy. Yet the militant, peaceful resistance of the peasant farmers and the political pressure of the southern governors made it difficult for Colombian authorities to continue making irresponsible accusations that these farmers were guerrilla collaborators and narcotraffickers, a common position taken after similar protests occurred in the mid-1990s in the departments of Caquetá and Guaviare. Perhaps more important, the protests and public denunciations represented a concrete example of how popular organizations were making connections between Washington's interventionist counterdrug policies and the impact that neoliberal reforms were having on the typical Colombian farmer.

While this has been going on in the agricultural sector, we have also seen an acceleration in the government's attempt to privatize vital state industries. Throughout the 1990s, the Inter-American Development Bank (IDB) promoted the privatization of public infrastructure, including its telecommunications, energy, and even its social security system, all as a way to address the government's budget woes. In doing so, as part of the "modernization" program of the neoliberal governments of Gaviria and, later, Ernesto Samper, tens of thousands of state workers were targeted with layoffs, while thousands of others were forced to tighten their belts and surrender salary increases and health care benefits. By the end of Gaviria's term, 113,000 public sector jobs had been cut, a process continued under Samper and Pastrana in the name of "modernizing" the state, reforms endorsed wholeheartedly by the United States.[9] Indeed, in 1999, Pastrana was forced to sign Colombia's first agreement with the International Monetary Fund (IMF), sparking further privatization, deeper austerity measures, and the massive dismissal of state workers. Throughout the 1990s, the proportion of Colombia's national budget directed toward servicing the debt increased every year, reaching 41 percent by 2001, thus making it by far the government's main priority, all at the expense of the typical Colombian worker.[10]

These policies have been consistently resisted by the largest trade union federations—the Central Unitaria de Trabajadores, or Unified Workers Central (CUT); Confederación General de

Trabajadores Democráticos, or the General Confederation of Democratic Workers (CGTD); and the Confederación de Trabajadores de Colombia, or Confederation of Colombian Workers (CTC). In May 2001, the CUT, the CGTD, and the CTC made a public commitment of collaboration in order to present "a unified workers front" against these and other policies deemed dangerous to Colombian public sector workers. The unified front was considered by many to be an unprecedented step after years of divisions within the trade union movement, divisions that led to a decline in their influence on the national scene in the 1980s and '90s.[11]

These points are worth raising within the context of U.S. policy for a number of reasons. For one, as already mentioned, many of the structural reforms affecting Colombian workers and peasants were forcefully encouraged by Washington, both as a precondition for favorable credits as well as a way to stimulate investment in the Colombian economy, particularly by U.S. multinationals. Second, while the United States strengthens the Colombian state security apparatus through aid packages such as *Plan Colombia*, it repeatedly gives lip service to the issue of human rights, an area that has clearly not improved for Colombian labor leaders.

Union activism, considered to be the most dangerous work in Colombia, has picked up despite the fact that between June 2001 and May 2002 at least 175 trade unionists were killed, 9 disappeared, 156 received death threats, 38 were kidnapped, and 4 were victims of arbitrary detentions by state security forces. In the past decade, 1,500 trade unionists have been killed, detained, forcibly disappeared, or forced to leave Colombia, lending credence to the CUT's description of this process as a "genocide whose purpose is to exterminate the union leadership and our organizations" in general.[12] All of this is carried out with complete impunity: Of the only 376 criminal investigations that have been conducted since 1986 involving violations against trade unionists, a full 321 remain in the preliminary stages, while only five people have been brought to justice.[13] In the vast majority of the cases, the alleged perpetrators are members of paramilitary groups who accuse labor activists of collaborating with the guerrillas.

In some instances, these attacks have been linked to multinational corporations whose subsidiaries have been threatened by union organizing in Colombia, including such names as British Petroleum and Coca-Cola. For example, according to the "Campaign to Stop Killer Coke," a national effort run by U.S.-based trade unions such as the United Steelworkers of America, the International Labor Rights Fund, and the Colombian labor union Sinaltrainal (food and beverage workers union), paramilitary groups have killed at least eight labor leaders who had been trying to unionize the bottling factories operated by Coca-Cola's Colombian subsidiaries, a charge Coca-Cola dismisses out of hand.[14] In the 1990s, British Petroleum (BP) was linked to the assassination of a number of union and community leaders who were against the privatization of the oil industry. These activists were highly critical of the contamination of the town of el Morro in the Casanare department, in the heart of Colombia's oil region, paying the ultimate price for daring to speak out against the practices of the oil company. While BP denied having any links with paramilitaries, it acknowledged using private security contractors in the area who were training Colombian police in counterinsurgency techniques.[15] Clearly, Colombia is the most difficult place in the world to do labor organizing. Neither *Plan Colombia* nor any of the other public policy pronouncements from Washington relating to Colombia have adequately addressed this harsh reality.

Economic Dimensions of *Plan Colombia*:
A Unifying Force for the Popular Movement

Before the tragic events of September 11, 2001, activists, scholars, and community leaders were pointing to *Plan Colombia* as the wake-up call needed by the popular movement to pick up its resistance against the economic and social policies of the government, as well as against growing U.S. interventionism. *Plan Colombia* may have been described publicly as a "counterdrug" program, but people in the popular movement could not help but think its primary purpose was to make the country safe for multinational economic interests while simultaneously militarizing the country even further. Dozens of articles and books critical of the plan were published; public forums and conferences were organized by community groups, universities, and human rights organizations throughout the country; and even anti–*Plan Colombia* rallies were held to address the concerns of many sectors of the popular movement. The people who were clamoring for the demilitarization of Colombian society saw the policy as Washington's open endorsement of more war.

Some argued that the economic dimensions of *Plan Colombia* had to be understood within the context of U.S. determination to dominate the hemisphere into the next century under the guise of the war on drug trafficking. Through the plan and its successor, the Andean Regional Initiative, Washington was looking to produce a change in the correlation of forces in the region favorable to the United States as well as the dominant classes of the region, backed up by the use of force and an expanded U.S. military presence in places like Ecuador, Peru, and Brazil in order to deal with some of the social instability in the region. Human rights activists saw this as a dangerous signal that, notwithstanding peace talks between the government and the FARC, an escalation in military confrontation was in the works. Economists and political scientists, meanwhile, made the links between these security measures and the eventual implementation of the Free Trade Area of the Americas (FTAA), expected to be in effect in 2005, a trade agreement characterized by further liberalization of the region's economies and the homogenization of the local currencies into the U.S. dollar.[16]

There was also concern among environmentalists and indigenous organizations that *Plan Colombia* and its "push into the south" was designed to create favorable conditions for the exploitation of the region's rich biodiversity by multinational biotechnology and genetic-engineering interests. Colombia's Amazon is said to have one of the most important and diverse reserves of plant and animal resources in the world. The "push into the south" was described by U.S. and Colombian officials as a way to fortify the state's presence in this region in order to combat illegal groups who were profiting from the drug trade. The formation and training of mobile counternarcotics brigades coinciding with intensive aerial fumigations of illicit crops were the main components of this strategy, alongside limited alternative development assistance.

Critics of the plan saw other motives driving U.S. officials and their Colombian counterparts. As they saw it, securing vast tracts of this territory from guerrillas, not to mention the indigenous and Afro-Colombian communities who held the title to many of these lands, would open the door for a bonanza in "bioprospecting" and the patenting of life that would surely follow, in essence expropriating traditional indigenous medicines and plants for multinational profit-making firms. In 1999, the president of the National Indigenous Organization of Colombia (ONIC), Abadio Green Stocell, visited the United States specifically to call attention to the effects these kinds of "economic" activities would have on the "cultural integrity of the indigenous communities of Colombia." The massive displacement that occurred in Putumayo in 2001 was just one of those effects.

Unfortunately, the exploitation of indigenous territories for the economic gains of outsiders is not something new, although the Colombian state has always argued that this is part of the cost of national progress and economic development. These projects include the construction of hydroelectric dams in territories inhabited by indigenous and Afro-Colombian communities; massive deforestation projects by both Colombian and multinational lumber companies; highway construction projects designed to facilitate transport of lumber and other raw materials to the country's two coasts; and extensive mineral mining projects. In most of these cases, communities have been forced to relocate, while leaders resisting the projects have been assassinated or disappeared. Social organizations like the ONIC have documented countless examples of how the state, in collaboration with private interests and with the backing of the armed forces, has not consulted with the communities before developing many of these projects, in direct violation of the Colombian Constitution. Indigenous and Afro-Colombian communities have resisted, but as a result they have suffered thousands of losses and massive displacement. Entire populations have disappeared. It is no coincidence that much of the recent displacement, particularly in Chocó, Córdoba, Antióquia, Putumayo, and Cauca, has taken place after paramilitary or guerrilla incursions into these strategic areas, lending credence to the argument that the displacement phenomenon is more than just a byproduct of the civil war between guerrillas and the state.[17]

And then, of course, there is the question of oil and protecting what Michael Klare described as "access to the most extensive oil deposits in the Western Hemisphere."[18] Colombia is the seventh-largest supplier of oil to the United States, and the potential for increased extraction has always attracted U.S.-based oil companies and their close friends in government. Oil production has soared over the last decade by 78 percent, from 100,000 barrels per day in the late 1980s to almost 850,000 by the end of the 1990s. Nevertheless, for a number of reasons, including the ongoing civil conflict and high levels of insecurity, only 20 percent of Colombia's potential oil regions have been explored. President Bush, following the lead of his predecessor President Clinton, has made it clear that the United States sees Colombia—and neighboring Venezuela—as so-called prime source countries for oil imports into the United States for the next twenty years. The region in the south along the border with Ecuador, not coincidentally where the bulk of *Plan Colombia*'s resources have been directed, is recognized as having important strategic petroleum reserves, much of it on indigenous territories. Critics of *Plan Colombia* and U.S. interventionism could not help but make the connection.

Oil Has Always Interested Uncle Sam

Given the history of oil exploration in Colombia and the indifference that multinationals and the government have shown toward indigenous communities in general, indigenous activists, environmentalists, and human rights workers had reason to be concerned about the links between *Plan Colombia* and oil interests. This history dates as far back as 1905, when the government began to dip into the country's petroleum deposits through contracts with private interests, both domestic and foreign. The so-called Mares Concession, signed over to the French-born Roberto de Mares by then-president Rafael Reyes and subsidized in part by the International Petroleum Company of Toronto, a subsidiary of Standard Oil, targeted the oil reserves alongside the Magdalena River in what is today the municipality of Barrancabermeja in the department of Santander. In less than two decades, through forced labor, the transmission of infectious diseases, and a complete transformation of their way of life, the entire population of the Yariguíe Indians was wiped out. Neither the government nor Standard Oil was ever forced to answer to what happened.[19]

Another egregious example was the Barco Concession of 1905, given to the Conservative General Virgilio Barco, a veteran of the War of a Thousand Days. Although it really didn't get off the ground until the late 1920s, the Barco Concession basically signed over the rights for exploration to the Gulf Oil Company, owned by Andrew Mellon, then U.S. Treasury Secretary. Resistance to oil exploration by the Motilón-Barí Indians led to Law 80 of 1931, which allowed the government to put "all the protection needed to repel attacks by the Motilón savages" at the disposal of oil companies, including "entire corps of the Armed Police or of the Public Force, as long as it was necessary."[20] Sixty years later, the Motilón tribe for which this law was originally directed had lost two-thirds of its ancestral territory and half its population.

In the early 1960s, in the department of Putumayo—the focal point for *Plan Colombia* in 2000—thousands of Ingá, Siona, and Kofan Indians were forced to relocate when the construction of roads and oil pipelines by Texas Oil and Ecopetrol—the state oil company—contaminated the communities' fresh water supplies. Back then, the population of the region was 65 percent indigenous, numbering about 13,000. Today, forty years after the development of oil in the area, indigenous people constitute less than 10 percent of the population.[21]

The ONIC and their allies in the environmental and human rights movement have made it a point not to forget this long history. They repeatedly point to protections spelled out in the Constitution of 1991 regarding the exploitation and control of the resources in their territories, protections included after years of militant struggle by the ONIC and its many regional affiliate organizations. They have been forced to confront the government almost daily on this issue. The massive resistance in the 1990s to California-based Occidental Petroleum's drilling plans in U'Wa territory in northeastern Colombia was seen as one minor victory in their movement. But the challenges have not stopped, not only from Occidental but from many other sources. Today, as paramilitaries wrest control of Putumayo and force further displacement of indigenous and peasant communities, it is clear that the militarization of the region sparked by *Plan Colombia* has made things much worse for the people inhabiting these areas. Ironically, because the government's aerial fumigation efforts and increasing paramilitary and guerrilla incursions are seen as the primary causes of the forced displacement, today nobody talks about the potential for oil exploration as a culprit in the social decay.

Plan Colombia After September 11

Before and during the implementation of *Plan Colombia*, popular organizations continued to raise all the issues just outlined as reasons to be skeptical about further U.S. meddling. The negative impact that neoliberal reforms were having on Colombian peasants and workers, the history of exploitation carried out by major U.S. multinationals, the dangerous effects of aerial eradication of drug crops, and the failure of the government to come up with viable alternatives for crop substitution were all presented as legitimate reasons to challenge the U.S.-backed drug war. Again and again, the issue of Colombian sovereignty was raised, with *Plan Colombia* seen as the ultimate surrender to U.S. authorities.

Colombian critics were joined in this resistance by U.S.-based human rights organizations, drug policy researchers, independent journalists, academics, and activists. Regularly published reports demonstrated how Washington's own stated objectives with *Plan Colombia* were not being met. Coca cultivation remained steady if it did not increase; the price of coca paste continued rising (providing peasant farmers with the incentive to continue cultivating); the street price of cocaine dropped as its purity increased; and, as I pointed out above, the security situation in Colombia was not improving by any stretch of the imagination.[22] As a result, the discrepancies inherent in Washington's Colombia strategy prior to September 11 were slowly being exposed on a number of fronts. That none of the stated goals behind U.S. policy were actually being met despite the massive influx of primarily military aid was becoming apparent. The emperor's drug war indeed had no clothes.

On the morning of September 11, 2001, Secretary of State Colin Powell was getting ready to fly to Colombia after a short visit to Peru, ostensibly to see first-hand how the *Plan Colombia* monies were being spent. Powell's regional tour was designed to capitalize on the fact that Colombia was in the news almost daily, and his high-profile visit to the southern department of Putumayo was to provide wonderful photo opportunities for both Colombian and U.S. news consumers. Of course, he was suddenly forced to change his plans due to the tragic events of the day. When the Twin Towers of the World Trade Center crumbled to the ground, it was clear that the United States would be forever changed. It also became readily apparent that, notwithstanding the fact that Colombia was suddenly off the media radar screen, these events would have a radical impact on the internal situation of the conflict and, more specifically, U.S. policy in Colombia.

Needless to say, in the wake of the attacks on Washington and New York, the growing public scrutiny of U.S. drug policy diminished. Within a few months, peace talks between the Colombian government and FARC rebels collapsed. Eventually, Alvaro Uribe was elected president on a platform of waging a total war against the rebels, that is, "terrorists." Furthermore, as I mentioned in the Introduction, U.S. military assistance to Colombia was no longer solely destined to fight drug trafficking but to carry out the international war against terrorism, a "policy shift" that found little opposition in Washington while being warmly embraced in Colombia. The floodgates were now opened for a continued flow of lethal military assistance from the United States that included a direct involvement of U.S. troops.

The foreign operations budget for 2003 included $538 million for Colombia, of which roughly 70 percent was for the military and police. Add to that the "antidrug" aid provided through the defense budget that involved construction, training, and intelligence, and the number approached half a billion dollars directed at military-security matters in one year alone, the most Colombia had ever received. Compare this to the $290 million pledged by the United States in 2002 to help rebuild Afghanistan, and one begins to see where Washington's priorities lie.[23]

To underscore the economic interests involved in the "revised" U.S. strategy after September 11, the Bush administration approved and deployed a multi-million-dollar military training program designed to protect an oil pipeline owned by U.S. multinational oil giant Occidental Petroleum. This is the same company that for years had been wanting to drill for oil in the ancestral lands of the indigenous U'Wa people, a traditional tribe of about 6,000 that had threatened to commit collective suicide rather than surrender its land to multinational oil exploration. The Caño-Limón pipeline carries an estimated 100,000 barrels of crude oil daily (about 35 million barrels a year) from the eastern department of Arauca across Colombia and into the Caribbean, where it eventually heads north for the oil-hungry U.S. market.

President Bush has pointed to oil production as a vital resource that will help the Colombian government fund its war against guerrillas. At the same time, as I mentioned above, his administration has made no attempts to disguise the fact that the United States sees Colombia as a vital source of imported oil over the next twenty years, at which time more than 62 percent of all U.S. oil consumption will be coming from foreign sources. Occidental Petroleum, whose officials have lobbied for years for the United States to become more involved in the conflict, made headway in 2001, thanks to its close links to the oil-friendly Bush team. Occidental was a major supporter of the U.S. aid package from the beginning, spending $350,000 lobbying Congress to ensure that the U.S. contribution to *Plan Colombia* was passed.[24] The company greeted with "considerable optimism" the lifting of restrictions on U.S. counterdrug aid to Colombia because it allowed the Pentagon to train Colombian military battalions in counterinsurgency tactics aimed at defending the oil pipeline from future guerrilla attacks. The price tag for the "Critical Infrastructure Brigade" was roughly $98 million, which added nearly $3 per barrel in costs to U.S. taxpayers, above the already 50 cents a barrel Occidental was paying in security costs.[25] Occidental spokesperson Larry Meriage told the *New York Times* that "you'll see more interest on the part of more companies" to do business in Colombia.[26] In January 2003, a contingent of about seventy U.S. Army Green Berets began arriving in Arauca for a series of training exercises to get the program started.

Indeed, the "oil war" is most evident today in the department of Arauca in northeastern Colombia. Early in his administration, President Uribe vowed to regain authority of the region, and in particular the town of Saravena, for years controlled by the FARC as well as the ELN. Uribe declared most of the department a special "rehabilitation and consolidation zone." The fact that U.S. Special Forces have been training troops of the army's 18th Brigade in counterinsurgency techniques, ostensibly to protect the pipeline, is evidence that both governments see this as a top priority in establishing order and combating terrorism. In July

2003, Uribe and his ministers held court for three days in Arauca, accompanied by 5,000 public security personnel. On one memorable morning, in a style reminiscent of the most telegenic of U.S. presidents, Uribe went out for a light jog, surrounded by the military's top brass, not to mention dozens of television cameras and news photographers. The highly orchestrated public relations gesture was designed to show to the Colombian people that security had been reestablished in the country, even in a volatile region such as Arauca. Ironically, less than ten hours after the presidential circus packed up its tent and returned to the capital, a car bomb exploded just yards away from where they had been meeting earlier in the day, wounding two people.

By all counts, the U.S. military training effort seemed to pay off, at least from the standpoint of protecting oil interests. From August 2002 to June 2003, there were only 83 reported attacks on the oil pipeline, a 41.1 percent drop from the same period the previous year, when the pipeline was blown up a total of 141 times.[27] Major William White, U.S. Special Forces chief in Arauca, told the *Wall Street Journal*, "Our mission is to train the Colombians to find, track down and kill the terrorists before they attack the pipeline."[28] This good news provided U.S. and Colombian officials with an incentive to continue and perhaps even expand the Pentagon's military role in Colombia. According to former U.S. Ambassador to Colombia, Anne Patterson, "there are more than 300 strategic infrastructure points for the United States in Colombia. . . . But first we'll see how this Caño Limón project goes."[29]

An Expanded U.S. Presence: "Advisors" or Combat Forces?

For some observers in early 2003, it appeared as if the United States was deliberately looking for a way to get more directly involved in the military entanglement that is Colombia. When a small, single-engine Cessna carrying U.S. "intelligence" officials fell in a guerrilla-controlled area in southern Colombia in February 2003, the Bush administration's indignation should have come as no surprise. Three U.S. officials were captured by FARC fighters in the incident, while two other men—a Colombian and an American—were found shot to death by the wreckage of the plane, the victims of what Colombian officials described as a guerrilla execution. As a result of this incident, Washington sent in a 150-man special-forces rescue team to help the Colombian army find the men, a unit that was permitted to participate in "offensive" military operations against the rebels. Thus began one of the largest known military deployments of U.S. forces in the forty-year history of the Colombian conflict.[30]

Anybody paying close attention might have asked, "What were these U.S. officials doing in that part of the country in the first place, knowing that they were in a war zone?" In fact, considering the situation of intense conflict and military battles, they should have expected the potential for some kind of direct action. Instead, the incident was made to look as yet another "despicable" act of terrorism carried out by the guerrillas against the United States, and the United States had to respond "with very strong retaliation."[31] The special forces unit introduced into the scene was the immediate response. This direct U.S. military presence in Colombia was the subject of a major public denunciation made by a group of retired military officers in March 2003. They charged the ministers of defense and foreign relations of not having fulfilled their constitutional duties by allowing "the national territory to be used by foreign forces without the express permission of the Colombian Congress."[32]

Therefore, as 2003 unfolded, elite U.S. forces were engaged in two of the hottest regions of the conflict: the oil-rich province of Arauca and the coca-growing region of Caquetá. This is without even considering the hundreds of "advisors" and private contractors engaged in countless undisclosed security and "training" operations throughout the country. Colombian human rights workers, peace activists, and popular movement leaders had warned of the potential for further U.S. meddling in the conflict when *Plan Colombia* was proposed in 1999. Three years, almost $2.5 billion, and hundreds of U.S. military "advisors" later, it becomes increasingly difficult to write them all off as alarmists.

Aerial Fumigations: Adding Fuel to the Drug-War Fire

In the wake of September 11, Washington also expanded the highly controversial program of aerial fumigations of coca plantations in southern Colombia, a policy that had been the focus of massive resistance on the part of the peasant coca farmers in previous years, as I pointed out earlier. For years, these peasants have argued that the chemicals used in the fumigation process damage food crops, threaten the health of their families, and pose a risk to the environment. The aerial fumigation of coca plantations has continued almost without interruption, despite the fact that human rights groups have cited it as a primary cause of the recent displacements of thousands of civilians from their homes who are forced to flee into neighboring Ecuador or other departments in southern Colombia.

The aerial eradication campaign has been a major point of contention with the FARC rebels, who demanded the issue be placed on the negotiating table during talks with President Pastrana. The FARC had called for an end to the fumigations until alternatives for the peasant farmers could be found, a proposal that was not seen as too credible in the midst of reports that the guerrillas were using the demilitarized zone to expand their own coca cultivations. In response to the governments' unwillingness to budge on the issue of fumigations, guerrillas repeatedly targeted the crop-dusting planes, winning the FARC very little support from the government for its proposals on crop substitution. This in turn led to an increase in right-wing para-military activity in the department of Putumayo, where according to various reports, "death squads roam the region freely, killing suspected rebel collaborators or anyone else who gets in their way. . . . Even the presence in [Puerto Asis] of a U.S.-trained counter-narcotics battalion has had no effect. . . . The area is becoming one of the world's deadliest places, with 128 reported homicides" in 2002.[33]

The spraying operation was supposed to coincide with development assistance for alternative crops, although the dispersal of funds has been limited to those farmers in Putumayo who signed "social pacts" in exchange for manual eradication of the illicit crops. According to peasant leaders and human rights activists, many farmers who signed the pact still had their land fumigated by the government, because the government failed to make distinctions between industrial plantations and small crops. People from the area argued this was fueling the anger and frustration of the community and was forcing people to leave their lands.[34]

In the absence of peace talks and in his campaign to broaden the war against the FARC, President Uribe has given American officials wide latitude in carrying out the spraying, which involves at least 18 crop-dusting planes and is expected to expand in the coming years. This is yet another example of Bogotá giving in to Washington's demands as conditions for further assistance, despite popular opposition. And although it can be seen as part of an overall counterdrug strategy, the fumigations add fuel to the fire of an already explosive situation of military conflict with the guerrillas in the south, while in actuality doing little to combat the drug problem.

In late February 2003, the White House Office of National Drug Control Policy issued a report saying that the strategy was finally "paying off," pointing to the fact that the amount of land being used to grow coca fell by 15 percent in 2002. What the optimistic press releases coming out of Washington failed to mention was that the previous year, the same office had reported the amount of coca cultivation in Colombia had actually increased almost 25 percent since *Plan Colombia* went into effect a year and a half earlier, a far cry from being on target for the "fifty-percent reduction in five years" goal laid out in the initial plan. Indeed, what the later numbers actually show is that, since 2000, there had been an overall increase in coca cultivation by roughly 10 percent, and the drop in 2002 by no means reflected a "turning point," the term used by John P. Walters, the director of national drug control strategy, to describe the news.[35] By the summer of 2003, the same office put out more numbers, saying that the Uribe government had successfully eradicated roughly 30 percent of all coca cultivations in Colombia in his first year in office. Both governments were openly taking credit for substantial gains in the drug war as measured by total crop acreage destroyed. What they conveniently underplayed in their accounting was that coca cultivation was gradually crossing the border once again into Peru and Ecuador, reversing the pattern that had occurred years earlier when the focus of U.S. eradication efforts was in those countries to the south, as well as in Bolivia.[36] Naturally, this kind of glaring contradiction attracted very little attention in the U.S. news media, perhaps because their collective eyes were glued to the unfolding war on Iraq, the latest and most dramatic stage of the war on terrorism. As stated in my Introduction, the drug issue had become less of a concern for the U.S. public.

Uribe-Bush: United in a Common Enterprise

It is safe to say that in the last fifteen years there has never been as close a relationship between the U.S. and Colombian governments as the one that exists today between presidents Bush and Uribe. The White House's insistence on linking the global war on terrorism to the Colombian conflict is evident in Bush's unconditional support for the Uribe government. Naturally this has been wholeheartedly embraced by Uribe, helping him in his unyielding drive to consolidate the nation's military and security apparatus, while implementing some of the most regressive economic reforms the country has seen in recent years. Perhaps it is no coincidence that simultaneously Bush and Uribe were enjoying favorable public opinion polls when it came to military and security concerns while being harshly criticized for their approach to economic matters.

Even in instances when differences have arisen between Bush and Uribe, in the long run these differences actually served the internal political interests of both governments. For example, in July 2003 the Bush administration announced it was freezing $5 million in aid to Colombia because of Uribe's failure to sign a bilateral accord relating to the Hague-based International Criminal Court (ICC). The Bush administration had pressured dozens of countries to sign the bilateral agreement, threatening to cut economic and military aid packages if they failed to comply. International human rights groups called the threats a clear example of how the United States considers itself to be above the law, describing it as Washington's attempt to make the ICC inoperable and ineffective.

The Pastrana government had initially endorsed the bilateral agreement to assure immunity for U.S. citizens involved in crimes against humanity or other war crimes committed in Colombia. But in an August 2002 letter to the new president, the Colombian Commission of Jurists said the agreement was tantamount "to authorizing any U.S. citizen to commit genocide or war crimes in our country and not be punished for it," thus "undermining the object and purpose of the treaty" (establishing the ICC).[37] Because of public domestic pressure on the matter,

Uribe scrapped the agreement, arguing that it was not necessary because a 1962 Colombian law already provided immunity for U.S. officials operating in the country. Meanwhile, the State Department made light of the differences of opinion between the two governments, expressing confidence that an agreement would be reached satisfactory to the interests of both countries. Nevertheless, when the punitive aid suspension was announced by Washington it was presented in the Colombian media as the first "direct confrontation" between Bush and Uribe, with Uribe getting high marks for standing up to the unilateralism of the United States. In this way, the Colombian leader was able to deflect growing internal criticism that he was under the direct command of George W. Bush. In September 2003, not surprisingly, an agreement was reached by both governments that resulted in the immunity Washington wanted for U.S. officials operating in Colombia. Ultimately, the bulk of U.S. military aid to Colombia was not affected, U.S. officials could rest assured now that their objectives vis-à-vis the ICC and Colombia were finally met, and President Uribe saved face at home by saying he stood up to the White House on this issue. As it turns out, everybody ended up winning, with the exception, of course, of the ICC.

In essence, both presidents are cut out of the same cloth, regularly expressing themselves publicly as if united in a common struggle against evil, using the same language, and even stage-managing their public appearances in similar ways so as to avoid any opposition. In both cases, there is little tolerance for public criticism. Popular resistance to the expanding war in Colombia (and the economic policies that facilitate that war) do not comfortably fall into either president's worldview that says clearly "you're either with us or against us." Be it the peasant farmer raising questions about the aerial fumigations, the indigenous leader protesting oil exploration, the public sector worker striking to maintain health benefits and a decent wage, the human rights attorney exposing the links between a local army captain and a right-wing death squad, or the independent political activist campaigning to open up democratic space in the country, the authoritarian process unfolding in Colombia is closing the possibilities for any of these groups to play a constructive role in the future of the country. Their voices and demands are unheard in Washington. It's as if they do not exist.

In many cases, the politically motivated violence directed against these popular sectors of Colombian society and the civilian population in general is manipulated by elected officials, both in Washington and Bogotá, to further justify a heavy-handed response to the problem. Security officials and politicians regularly point to the guerrillas, that is, the "terrorists," as being the primary culprits of the violence, notwithstanding evidence to the contrary. For example, it was only in August 2001 that the U.S. State Department finally placed the right-wing paramilitary organization, AUC, on its list of terrorist organizations, despite years of public denunciations by human rights groups. Some said it was because Washington could no longer ignore the atrocities being carried out by the AUC. Others argued the decision was a public relations move just weeks before Powell's scheduled September 11 visit in order to sell Washington's Andean Regional Initiative to a skeptical Colombian public.

Notwithstanding the recent "terrorist" designation for the AUC, nor the Justice Department's indictment of Castaño and the AUC leadership, the strongest public condemnations by U.S. officials continue to be reserved for the left-wing guerrillas, the greatest threat to Colombian democracy. For example, in a House of Representatives resolution debated in March 2002, the FARC, ELN, and AUC were all mentioned, but the FARC and ELN were cited eleven times for their roles in terrorist activities such as kidnappings, murder, and destruction of property. The AUC were cited five times, with two mentions referring specifically to "*individual members* of Colombia's security forces" who "have collaborated with illegal paramilitary organizations by . . . *in some instances* allowing such organizations to pass through roadblocks, sharing tactical information with such organizations, and providing such organizations with supplies and ammunition" (emphasis added). The other mention of the AUC gives credit to the Colombian government for making "progress in its efforts to combat and capture members of illegal paramilitary organizations and [taking] positive steps to break links between individual members of the security forces and such organizations." This runs counter to numerous studies that describe the close ties that continue between paramilitary and army elements as a systematic counterinsurgency strategy, and that attribute more than three-quarters of all human rights atrocities carried out in Colombia to these right-wing death squads.[38]

Even when both the left-wing guerrillas and the right-wing paramilitaries are given equal weight by administration officials in terms of their terrorist credentials, the resulting U.S. response remains the same, as when Otto Reich defended Bush's support for Uribe on the eve of Uribe's inauguration: "We're not going to engage in counterinsurgency in Colombia," he said, "because there is no counterinsurgency in Colombia. What you have is three terrorist groups that operate as organized-crime families, except they wear combat fatigues and they have a lot of people and some very high-powered weapons. . . . These are not insurgents. These are criminals. These are terrorists . . . and Colombia is a democratic country, freely elected. It's a friend, and we're going to support them."[39]

Therefore, terrorism becomes very narrowly defined in the Colombian context, a definition that suits perfectly the military and political objectives of both governments. The FARC, the ELN, and the AUC are all classified as terrorist groups by the United States and Colombia. Given the current global climate of zero tolerance for terrorist violence, and the deterioration of the conflict in Colombia whereby such actions have become increasingly common, it is not completely unreasonable for the United States to embrace and support the hard-line approach adopted by Uribe. But as Colombian political scientist Eduardo Pizarro writes, to classify an organization as "terrorist" is fundamentally "a political decision that has limited foundations in rigorous academic analysis." In every case, the designation will be valid only so long as the government making the designation finds it useful.[40] After all, one does not negotiate with terrorists. Therefore, the double standard of treatment given to the rebels and the paramilitaries should cause any objective observer considerable concern. What this may mean for the long-term peace and security of Colombia is extremely alarming, although it doesn't appear to be too troubling for U.S. officials.

Indeed, the policies applied by Uribe have been applauded repeatedly by U.S. officials, who often like to take credit for their apparent success. For example, General James T. Hill, chief of the U.S. Southern Command, said on the first anniversary of Uribe's presidency, "In my opinion, Colombia has been a good investment for United States' policy and our resources."[41] He was not talking about the last twenty years of drug war failures, but rather the small gains of Uribe's mandate mentioned earlier. Democracy is being served in Colombia like never before. If we stay the course, things can only get better.

Of course, Gen. Hill does not have to concern himself with the loss of life that can be guaranteed in the coming years as the war against the guerrillas unfolds. He also need not pay attention to the tens of thousands of workers who will be forced to accept salary cuts and service reductions in order to help pay for the war. And, yes, peasant farmers will continue to be displaced from the countryside, either directly by the violence and the fumigations, or by the rapid influx of imported agricultural products that can be expected as Colombia gets incorporated into the Free Trade Area of the Americas. But these are internal matters not of importance to the United States. After all, a global war on terrorism has to be won. If anything, the conceptual foundations of *Plan Colombia* have to be expanded even further to build on the "gains made so far against terrorism and narcotrafficking, the economy and human rights."[42]

In the United States, meanwhile, think tanks and human rights groups, including the Washington Office on Latin America (WOLA), and the Latin America Working Group (LAWG), continue to insist that, three years after the implementation of *Plan Colombia*, the situation is not as rosy as U.S. officials so often like to paint it. Citing an increase in the number of internally displaced people, a rise in coca cultivation in neighboring countries, and setbacks in judicial reform and the protection of human rights, the groups gave *Plan Colombia* an "F" on the occasion of its third anniversary. Perhaps their biggest concern was the manner in which U.S. policy has pushed aside the possibility of a negotiated solution to the decades-long conflict in favor of more direct military confrontation with the guerrillas.[43] Whether or not their opinions will be heard is another matter entirely.

Going back to Antonio Caballero's observation mentioned at the outset of this chapter, perhaps we can now add a third "decision" made by the United States that will have profound effects on the future of Colombia. That "decision," of course, was to expand its war on terrorism, launched in the aftermath of September 11, into every corner of the globe, including Colombia. As in the past with the anticommunist crusade and the drug war, the latest "decision" has been welcomed universally by Colombian military authorities, political leaders, and its economic elite. And once again, opposition to the "decision" is marginalized, if not outright ignored. As we will see in the next chapter, the U.S. news media have fallen right in line.

6

Colombia in the News:
Structural Dangers in a Post-9/11 World

Considering that most people develop an understanding of the world through the news media, examining how the principal U.S. news organizations tend to report on Colombia is a good place to begin to grapple with the many misconceptions that exist today about the country. Over the years, I have been invited to countless forums, conferences, seminars, and workshops to discuss the situation in Colombia. On almost every occasion, I am forced to begin by breaking through the clouded picture that people tend to have about Colombia, which I believe stems from how the complexities of the conflict are presented in news reports, features, editorials, and opinion pieces in U.S. mainstream media outlets.

Colombia has generated considerable news coverage over the years, particularly since the late 1980s and early 1990s, when, as mentioned in chapter 5, the first President Bush launched his all-out drug war. Back in the mid- to late 1980s, the focus was primarily on the urban terror campaign being waged by the Medellín cartel of Pablo Escobar and the movement against extraditing drug kingpins to the United States to stand trial. The peace agreements signed by the rebel group M-19, as well as the Constituent Assembly in 1991 that rewrote Colombia's antiquated Constitution, generated very little interest when compared to the bombs detonating almost daily in the streets of Bogotá and Medellín. Attention picked up again in the mid-1990s when the issue of human rights restrictions on U.S. aid began to make some headlines, at the same time that the Colombian president, Ernesto Samper Pizano, was being accused of accepting campaign contributions from the Cali cocaine cartel. Later, when *Plan Colombia* was being debated in Congress and peace talks were launched between the FARC and the government, Colombia once again started to appear regularly in the news.

Over the last fifteen years or so, it's safe to argue that the patterns in coverage have remained consistent: The major U.S. news media for the most part echo the position of the U.S. government, present the vast array of complex issues affecting Colombia within the context of U.S. interests in the region, frame the Colombia "story" in a one-dimensional way that portrays the Colombian government as a "good friend" of the United States that is under siege from narcotraffickers and terrorists, and target the left-wing guerrillas and their links to the drug trade as the primary threat to the security of both Colombia and the United States, although this final trait is more characteristic of the last three or four years of coverage.

Because this covers a vast time frame, one can easily charge me for being too general in my critique, or perhaps even accuse me of oversimplifying many years of different coverage that collectively represents a broad range of diversity in perspectives and ideas. This is a fair argument. The *New York Times* is clearly not the same thing as the *Washington Times*, National Public Radio presents a more nuanced picture than CBS Radio, *60 Minutes* does a considerably better job in investigating stories than Fox News. I usually refrain from making sweeping comments about "the media," considering that indeed many media are operating with different missions, using distinct technologies and serving a broad range of functions and constituencies. With all the media outlets that exist, obviously many examples exist of exceptionally strong, responsible reportage that places the conflict in a proper historic context while exposing the varied interests behind U.S. and Colombian state policy, both in the commercial-corporate and the independent media. Clearly, to say that "the media" cover Colombia in any particular way can be risky.

It makes much more sense to take a clearly defined time frame, choose specific media outlets, and look for the patterns that come up again and again before making any judgments about "the media." In light of my broader argument that the U.S. and Colombian governments have, in direct partnership, expanded their approach to the internal conflict to fit it comfortably within the framework of the global war on terrorism, it makes sense to observe how the mainstream media in the United States have covered Colombia since the attacks on September 11, 2001. From there, we can begin to examine whether or not the media are once again guilty of oversimplifying the picture for the U.S. news-consuming public, ultimately benefiting Washington's present policy.

For example, let's consider the one-year period between September 11, 2001, and September 11, 2002. This was a period when much of the world's attention was on the U.S. response to the attacks on Washington and New York. Needless to say, issues of war, security, and terrorism were in the news daily. As for Colombia, despite not being the primary focus of media scrutiny, it could still be considered to have been a major issue of concern for Washington policymakers during this time. The concise one-year time frame also allows us to avoid mixing up the complexities of the changing dynamics that have characterized Colombian politics, the civil conflict, and its relationship to the United States over the last fifteen years, all of which have evolved considerably.

Let's specifically take into account nine major media outlets: the *Washington Post, New York Times, Boston Globe, San Francisco Chronicle, The Economist, Newsweek, U.S. News & World Report, Gannett News Service,* and *CNN.*[1] It is fair to say that, collectively, these prestigious newspapers, magazines, and news services represent the cream of the crop of the United States news and information media. Although only one is given the lofty title "paper of record," clearly they all have considerable influence, and their editorial content generates a massive echo throughout all the other media in the country, print and broadcast, as well as online. This is not to mention the influence that these outlets have on the Colombian media as well; it is not uncommon for a story reported in *Newsweek* or an editorial printed in the *New York Times,* for example, to find its way to the front pages of *El Tiempo* or on the news talk programs of Colombia's radio and television networks. Therefore, if we were to do a systematic quantitative as well as a qualitative analysis of these nine outlets, it would be safer to make the argument "the media cover Colombia in such and such a way." What comes up is rather instructive.

In the year after the terrorist attacks on the World Trade Center, Colombia appeared in 118 pieces within these nine outlets, in a wide range of story themes. These included feature reports, news blurbs, and editorials on drug trafficking, human rights violations, domestic/international terrorism, and regional economic and security issues. In the weeks after September 11, 2001, a number of stories focused on the implications of the attacks for Colombian citizens in the United States and in Colombia. As mentioned in the previous chapter, the breakdown in talks between the government and the FARC got a lot of coverage, as did the presidential elections of May 2002. Colombia's relationship to the crisis in Venezuela and other regional matters also appeared regularly (see Table 6.1).

Table 6.1 Colombia in the News, Separated by Time Periods

	Sept. 11, 2001– Nov. 2001	Dec. 2001– Feb. 2002	Mar. 2002– May 2002	June 2002– Sept. 11, 2002
Washington Post	3	16	15	3
New York Times	12	10	22	8
Boston Globe	1	2	2	2
San Francisco Chronicle	1	1	3	1
The Economist	1	3	4	1
Newsweek	—	—	2	1
U.S. News & World Report	—	1	—	—
Gannet News Service	—	—	1	—
CNN	1	—	1	—
Total	19	33	50	16

Orientation: Picking Sides?

Because of the journalistic news values of objectivity and fairness, at times it is difficult to adequately analyze quantitatively the slant of the media coverage, especially when talking about hard news stories and feature reporting. It should be pointed out that journalists tend to cover themselves from charges of partisanship by closely attributing specific accusations from one side against another while depending on interviews with government officials and/or policy experts as their primary research.[2] The views expressed, therefore, are not their own but others'. They're simply "reporting" on what is being said. This also allows them to, at the very least, acknowledge the existence of alternative interpretations or extenuating circumstances.

In the majority of cases in the one-year sample, however, coverage of the dynamic conflict in Colombia is exceedingly one-dimensional. The vast majority of the newspaper articles tend to put emphasis on the negative aspects of the FARC and the positive aspects of the Colombian government, reflecting the double standard I described in chapter 5. Indeed, taken as a whole, a "good guy"/"bad guy" binary emerges, with the Colombian government as the former and the FARC as the latter. For example, in a January 11, 2002 *New York Times* article, Christopher Marquis writes, "privately, experts said Mr. Pastrana has been under considerable pressure—including influenced by the United States—to take a tougher line against the rebels. . . . A Senior State Department official, Marc Grossman, told Mr. Pastrana of American concerns that the FARC was using the demilitarized zone to train terrorists, hide kidnapping victims and raise money by trafficking in drugs."[3] Here the responsibility of the impending failure of the peace talks falls squarely on the FARC. The reader is left with the assumption that the government has done nothing wrong in the process itself, and with the exception of a brief line at the end of the article, ignores the role the right-wing paramilitaries may have played in the failing peace dialogue, an issue I already described at length in chapter 4. This tendency is repeated throughout the one-year monitoring period.

In fact, in almost every article—both within and outside the sample—I tracked down in the weeks following the breakdown of peace talks between the FARC and the Pastrana administration in February and March 2002, the FARC is always mentioned first in terms of its involvement in drug trafficking and terrorist activity, and the ELN guerrillas and the AUC are mentioned later. One typical example was in George Gedda's *Associated Press* dispatch on March 7, 2002, reprinted in the *Washington Post*, where the reporter writes: "Of the three Colombian [terrorist] groups, the leftist FARC rebels are seen as the biggest threat to Colombian democracy," without provid-

Table 6.2 Colombia in the News—Type of Articles

	Blurb[a]	Editorial	Feature
Washington Post	6	5	25
New York Times	6	7	40
Boston Globe	—	1	6
San Francisco Chronicle	1	5	—
The Economist	1	8	—
Newsweek	—	—	3
U.S. News & World Report	—	—	1
Gannet News Service	—	—	1
CNN	1[b]	1[b]	—
Total	15	27	76

a. A "blurb" is an article of 250 words or less, found typically in World Briefs.

b. CNN segments are not "articles," so they are classified a bit awkwardly.

ing attribution.[4] The long history of the AUC's attacks on democracy is completely ignored.

Again, because of journalists' attempts at objectivity, it is often extremely difficult to quantify this progovernment bias in feature writing and hard news reports. However, editorials can more easily be analyzed for their bias in picking sides due to their acknowledged subjectivity. Therefore, it is useful to break down the one-year sample by article type, seeking to extract a sense of where the overall sympathies tend to lie, at least in these nine media outlets (see Table 6.2).

Focusing on editorials alone, it is possible to categorize these pieces into two main groups: (1) those sympathetic to the Colombian government and critical of the FARC, and (2) those against the government and, in turn, U.S. policy. It is not surprising that no editorials, or features for that matter, are sympa-

Table 6.3 Orientation/Subject of Newspaper Editorials

	Pro-Govt./ Current U.S. Policy	Anti-govt./ Current U.S. Policy	Other[a]
Washington Post	4	1	—
New York Times	4	1	2
Boston Globe	1	—	—
San Francisco Chronicle	1	4	—
The Economist	6	—	2
Newsweek	—	—	—
U.S. News & World Report	—	—	—
Gannet News Service	—	—	—
CNN	1	—	—
Total	17	6	4

a. These editorials mentioned Colombia but were about other conflicts such as the temporary coup d'état in Venezuela or the drug war in Peru.

thetic to the FARC or any of the other nonstate combatants. Of the twenty-seven editorials tracked, only six were somewhat critical of the Colombian government or U.S. foreign policy. Four of these six came from one news source, the *San Francisco Chronicle* (see Table 6.3).

In contrast, seventeen of the twenty-seven editorials can be characterized as being pro–Colombian government/U.S. government or anti-FARC. These pieces are extremely diverse in content, ranging from opinion articles tacitly supporting the government as a "lesser of two evils" (which we can classify as "Support with Strings," Table 6.4) to pieces ignoring or sidestepping all excesses of the Colombian government while advocating for more intense U.S. involvement in the conflict ("Support without Strings," Table 6.4). An example of the former would be a *New York Times* edi-

Table 6.4 Orientation within Progovernment Editorials

	Pro-govt./Current U.S. Policy	
	Support with Strings	Support without Strings
Washington Post	1	3
New York Times	3	1
Boston Globe	1	—
San Francisco Chronicle	1	—
The Economist	3	3
Newsweek	—	—
U.S. News & World Report	—	—
Gannet News Service	—	—
CNN	—	1
Total	9	8

torial on March 9, 2002, titled "The War in Colombia Intensifies," wherein the editor insists that a tougher stance against the FARC is a "justified move" and that the Colombian "government's hand was ultimately forced," yet also stresses:

> Congress must resist the temptation to use America's war on terror elsewhere as an excuse to more deeply involve the United States in this decades-long conflict. The United States can best help the Colombian people by conditioning any further military aid on an improvement in the army's human rights record.[5]

In contrast, an example of the latter, that is, unconditional support for U.S. and Colombian government policy, can be found in a January 14, 2002, *Washington Post* editorial titled "Remember Colombia," in which the author writes:

Though both the [Bush] administration and Congress are properly concerned about the [Colombian] army's record of human rights violations, the real point of the policy has been to limit U.S. involvement in a fight against extremists. . . . Such logic was typical before Sept.11; now it seems glaringly out of place. . . . The administration should abandon its attempt to distinguish counternarcotics from counterinsurgency aid to Colombia. If the United States can support governments and armies battling extremists in Central and Southeast Asia . . . it ought to be able to give similar aid to an embattled democratic government in Latin America.[6]

Another interesting characteristic of the many opinion pieces written about Colombia during this period is the repeated reference to the threat Colombian democracy faces from the guerrillas, without any critical analysis. The false perception about Colombian democracy was printed in just about every editorial I found in the U.S. media in the days after the peace talks between the FARC and Pastrana government broke down in February 2002. Indeed, it's almost as if they were written by the same person, as one can see from these three editorials taken from smaller publications that were not part of my larger sample:

- From the *Dallas Morning News*: "Given the administration's commitment to fighting 'terrorism with a global reach' and to defending democracy in the Americas, it is difficult to ignore the Colombians' plea. The rebels' reach is certainly global in the sense that they participate in narcotics trafficking that undermines the United States and other American republics. They are certainly a dire and urgent threat to one of the Americas' *oldest democracies*" (emphasis added).

- From the *South Florida Sun-Sentinel*: "A 40-year conflict intensifies. Now the disappearance of a presidential candidate, in the midst of a campaign, points to civil meltdown. Colombia is a *troubled democracy* fighting for its survival" (emphasis added).

- From the *Washington Times*: "Considering the fact that *Colombia is the oldest democracy* in Latin America, the Bush administration must take all of FARC's recent dastardly deeds seriously and act accordingly—both for U.S. national security and to help the Colombian government better protect its citizens" (emphasis added).[7]

Where's the Bias?

It is clear that, from a quantitative perspective, U.S. media outlets disproportionately disseminate information with a distinctively pro-Colombian government slant, particularly in editorial content. This should come as no surprise, considering the tendency of the U.S. news media in general to follow the lead of government officials and policymakers when reporting on national security issues. Obviously Colombia is a strong U.S. ally in the region. It is a regular recipient of substantial amounts of military and economic assistance, as I have already pointed out. It is a country where major U.S. economic interests have a lot at stake. Reporters covering Colombia are naturally going to reflect these broader trends and follow the lead from those who are shaping policy. This inevitably prevents them from delving deeper into other areas that perhaps would illuminate the nuances of the current situation on the ground far more profoundly.

I have spoken to numerous journalists covering Colombia for a broad range of media outlets who simply say to me, "my editor would never be interested in this story," when discussing things like indigenous mobilizations against the government or efforts of the independent peace movement. Those stories are quite simply not newsworthy when put up against a U.S. congressional delegation visiting the coca-growing south, or another high-profile kidnapping carried out by the FARC. Again, we should be wary of clumping all reporters into the same category of bandwagon or press-release journalism. Over the years, a number of excellent exposés have been published about human rights abuses, the environmental and social impact oil exploration is having in particular areas of the country, and the links between the Colombian army and right-wing paramilitaries. Some of these articles appear in the sample. But clearly, they are the exception, not the rule.

To fully understand the role of the American media in framing the issues of the war in Colombia, we must recognize other, more subtle biases. For example, in the articles tracked in the sample, there is a pattern of using superficial references to excesses carried out by both sides of the conflict, but with significant spatial differentiation. In the majority of cases, articles list, at length, excesses committed by the FARC, then in sparing terms note that similar, or indeed often worse, acts were committed by the paramilitary forces. For example in the same *New York Times* article cited earlier, "U.S. Supports Colombian on Ultimatum to Rebels," reporter Christopher Marquis catalogs the numerous charges against the FARC leveled by the U.S. government. Although he notes in the last paragraph that incursion into former rebel territory "if mishandled, could result in a . . . human rights 'disaster' if rebels hold their ground or right-wing paramilitaries and their military allies turn their wrath on the 90,000 civilians living in the zone," the vast majority of the article (fourteen of the fifteen paragraphs) focuses on the negative acts of the FARC.[8] These first fourteen paragraphs contain no mention or indication of the serious questions raised about government and paramilitary actions and indeed participation in the same acts. What emerges is an article essentially shielding itself from allegations of one-sidedness, and yet it focuses more than 93 percent of its content on one side's negative actions.

In addition to spatial biases, articles in the sample tended to reveal bias in word choice as they related to descriptions of actions of the combatants. In an April 25, 2002, *Washington Post* article, Karen DeYoung writes, "In addition to its involvement with drug trafficking, the FARC increasingly uses *terror tactics*, including blowing up energy infrastructure, placing car bombs on urban streets and kidnapping civilians" (emphasis added).[9] Again, as in the majority of articles about the FARC, the group is described in terms of terrorism and the victimization of innocent civilians. This contrasts significantly with another article by DeYoung, on May 2, 2002, in which the focus is ostensibly criticism of the Colombian government and paramilitaries. The author writes, "[Senator] Leahy and others have long been concerned that the *zeal* of the U.S. and Colombian military in combating the . . . FARC, has led them to turn a *blind eye* [to paramilitary activities]" (emphasis added).[10]

In these two articles, a number of implicit, but nonetheless very present, contentions are made, which, when contrasted, reveal the author's own bias. On the one hand, we are presented with a portrayal of FARC activities directly labeled as "terror tactics," which by extension labels the group itself terrorist. On the other hand, excesses committed by, or in support of, the Colombian government are attributable to the "zeal" of these agents. Furthermore, actions of the paramilitary, estimated by Colombian and United States–based human rights groups to be responsible for 70–75 percent of human rights abuses in the country, committed as an extension of the government's response to the FARC, are explained merely as the result of a lack of oversight, or a "blind eye," as opposed to active collusion.

We also have to consider that even when an article makes overtures toward giving balance, the framing of the article itself can tell a different story. In a different *New York Times* article by Marquis, titled "U.S. to Explore Aid to Colombia, Citing Threat of Terrorism," the author attempts to distance himself from clearly partisan views expressed by "officials" in government through the use of syntax, such as quotation marks, and direct attribution. Marquis chronicles some impressively candid and telling viewpoints, for example quoting an unnamed official:

> "People [in the government] are interested in considering a move from counternarcotics to counterterrorism, rather than counterinsurgency" . . . the official conceded that the distinction was largely "just a change of words," but he said it would have an important role in public perceptions. . . . "I don't think anyone in Congress is going to stand up and say, "Hey let's do some counterinsurgency."[11]

Using these and similar quotes in other articles, Marquis provides vivid demonstrations of the extent to which U.S. government officials have intentionally manipulated and blurred the language and concepts that frame how the war in Colombia is understood in the United States. However, he fails to go beyond a vague implication that there *could* be another fundamentally different interpretation of the crisis. In other words, through the framing of the article itself, the author accepts and indeed implicitly endorses the broader narrative of the government, including its definitions of what constitutes "terror" and how and why the government is fighting against it, issues I have addressed at length in earlier chapters.

What we see in this one-year sample of articles is straightforward and somewhat self-evident, and can be applied to the news coverage of just about every major national and international issue. That is, the U.S. media's presentations of the war in Colombia have been profoundly colored by the post–September 11 political environment in the United States. It is essential to establish this before we begin any attempt to analyze information flows about the war in a qualitative manner. The war in Colombia has persisted for roughly four decades, with varying degrees of U.S. involvement. The U.S. war on "terror" can be traced to September 11, 2001, a period of approximately two years. Through its long duration, the Colombian conflict clearly has developed a number of political, class, and ethnic undercurrents that continue to influence its trajectory, details of which I've tried to illuminate at length. In recent months, the apparent shift in U.S. security policy and international diplomacy has clearly become another factor in the armed conflict, affecting internal tactics of Colombian actors and how these actions are spun to the outside world. Indeed, everything else would appear to be irrelevant.

It is undeniable that the attacks of September 11 have profoundly affected the way that Americans view the outside world, and consequently we can expect that the media will reflect this change. However, we must recognize that viewing September 11 as a punctuating mark in all other conflicts can lead to a fundamentally flawed representation of the situation on the ground. The collective narrative of the causes and effects of our own tragedy has led to attempts to fit external conflicts into broadly generalized and highly ideological worldviews. In the context of Colombia, three distinct tendencies in coverage can perhaps be linked to structural flaws in the way the media report and explain external conflicts: (1) a lack of focus on history; (2) the absence of class, race, and ethnicity; and (3) the tendency to fill these information vacuums with ideological anecdotes and metaphors.

A War with No History or Roots

Much of the problem with American media coverage of the Colombian civil war lies not in what is reported, but in what isn't. The United States–based global news media tend toward heavy coverage of excesses of the FARC while paying less (if any) attention to government collusion with the paramilitaries and AUC death squads. While government corruption is occasionally reported, it is usually presented as a localized matter, or something that will be weeded out with the new, more efficient people in charge. When the potential for corporate greed is reported, as was the case with Occidental Petroleum's controversial plan to drill for oil in sacred indigenous land, it is presented as an aberration, far removed from the U.S. government and its perceived interests in the country. In fact, very rarely are the dots connected. This is a major impediment to fair and balanced reporting, explored in more detail below. Throughout the sample, however, perhaps the most profound, if less obvious, absence in media coverage was a fully compelling narrative of how the conflict itself began.

Clearly, functioning within the form of a news article, it would be extremely difficult if not impossible to elaborate on the numerous roots of this conflict. Dozens of books have been written about Colombia in recent years, each of which might differ in terms of their respective interpretations of the origins of today's civil war. One cannot expect journalists trained in the art of the inverted pyramid to spend too much time trying to sort through this muddled history. However, we must recognize that in the absence of an alternative, news coverage inevitably reverts to the prevalent narrative of the broader media. In the case of Colombia, what we see is an ongoing narrative of the past fifteen years that posits the idea that the internal political-social and military conflict is about narcotics trafficking seeping into every sector of Colombian life, with unbridled terrorism being a direct manifestation of this phenomenon.

Interestingly, FARC actions in recent years have to some extent actually fit within this mold, as it has increasingly come to rely on profits derived from the drug trade and kidnapping to sustain its activities. However, this cannot explain why the war started in the first place, before the ascendancy of cocaine as a major cash crop or the popular concept of what constituted terrorism, nor why the government of Colombia has been unable to rouse enough popular support to effectively route out this insurgency.

I should point out that this is an extremely delicate argument to make, especially in the current context. Many commentators in Colombia, including some considered to be progressive, have discarded the historical roots of the conflict in their analysis of the contemporary conflict. Government officials and the Colombian dominant classes often accuse people making the "historical roots" argument as being, at best, idealistic dreamers out of touch with reality and, at worst, open apologists for terrorists.[12] But it is my contention that independent, objective journalists cannot avoid approaching Colombia from a historical perspective. Otherwise they will ultimately fail to adequately address the manner in which history in Colombia finds a way to repeat itself, especially in terms of the countless government efforts to win the war through increased militarization, the suspension of civil liberties, and the expansion of repressive tactics in the name of security, all to no avail. The U.S. historical role in this process is also conveniently left off the table for further scrutiny.

An Absence of Class, Race, and Ethnicity

The conflict in Colombia has been profoundly shaped by identity-grounded conflicts linked to political participation, class, and race/ethnicity. These differences cannot be simplified into binaries and indeed cannot fully explain the conflict. Conversely, however, it is impossible to understand the conflict without recognizing their influence. Yet despite their clear influence on the war, class, race, and ethnicity are largely invisible in the sample. The absence of these factors can lead to simplistic and often misleading explanations and interpretations of events.

During the Colombian elections in May 2002, the nine media outlets tracked in the sample constantly refer to the Colombian voting public as a cohesive unit that we are told has come to fully back a hard-line approach towards the FARC. Implicitly, this would claim that class allegiance has lost salience. Throughout the electoral campaign, and when peace talks between Pastrana and the FARC were on the ropes, we saw much of the same. So, for example, in an article entitled "After a Killing, Colombian Leader Has to Decide on Peace Talks," the *New York Times'* Juan Forero quotes a poll that says 87 percent of Colombians do not want the peace plan, and then he proceeds to interview a Bogotá-based lawyer who expressed displeasure with President Pastrana's talks with the FARC.[13] Surely Mr. Forero could have found a more representative sample to give the reader a sense of what the Colombian "public" is thinking.

In fact, polls must always be questioned, especially within the context of a civil conflict such as Colombia's. First we must be skeptical about the range of locations across the country in which people are being polled—a peasant farmer in Putumayo, for example, will most likely have a different take on the war than a small business owner in Medellín, although the small business owner is much more likely to be contacted for a national poll because of the communication technology at his disposal, as well as the tendency of pollsters and journalists to avoid people not considered to be within their own social reach. In fact, every poll published by *El Tiempo* contains a small box that describes the polling sample. Not surprisingly, they include people contacted by phone in Bogotá, Medellín, Cali, Barranquilla, and Bucaramanga, the five largest cities in the country. One begs to ask, What about the people in southern Cauca, in the Sierra Nevada of Santa Marta, in the jungles of Caquetá, or in the fishing towns of Chocó? Or could it be that their opinions really do not matter?

There is also the reliability of the poll responses themselves, given the fact that threats and intimidation make up a natural part of the landscape in Colombia. People are not likely to be forthcoming when complete strangers ask them to address certain matters, especially relating to national security. So in terms of both the generalizability of the results, as well as the validity of the polling tactics, we must take any poll published in Colombia with a healthy dose of skepticism. Indeed, over the years, public opinion polls have been used again and again in Colombia by the armed forces and their supporters in the monopoly media to promote a more hard line agenda, a fact that very rarely gets noted in news reports written by journalists like Forero.[14] Taking this into consideration, it becomes somewhat suspect when a news magazine reports that public opposition to Uribe's highly restrictive security measures implemented after taking office "is so far largely restricted to trade union leaders and human rights groups," as *The Economist* pointed out in an August 17, 2002, article entitled "State of Commotion."[15]

In a *Washington Post* article titled "Colombia Elects a Hard Liner on Fighting Rebels," Scott Wilson describes election victor Alvaro Uribe as a "bookish former provincial governor," whose "security-first approach" not only "fits more naturally with the Bush administration's war on terrorism," but also successfully united Colombians. Citing "guerrilla attacks on rural towns . . . and kidnappings of Colombia's elite," Wilson contends "Uribe's support, once confined to Colombia's conservative elite, has deepened ever since."[16]

Although it is clear that recent actions by the FARC caused it to lose many sympathizers, it is also essential to recognize the continued salience of class in a country with major wealth disparity. Certainly Uribe's victory was historic in terms of Colombian elections, garnering more than 52 percent of the vote and thereby not requiring a runoff. But the abstention rate of 54 percent—to Wilson's credit, mentioned in his report—was the highest in Colombia's history, begging the question: Is the country truly "united" behind Uribe? Indeed, it is interesting to note that within the whole sample, this article is the only one that implies a (historic) division of Colombian society along the lines of class when it quotes Uribe in the second-to-last line saying education is "the most efficient path to an egalitarian nation where no one is condemned by their economic status."[17]

These weaknesses can likewise be seen (or not seen) in the absence of reference to the trade-union movement. Although some articles do reference the fact that the paramilitary death squads and, by extension, the Colombian government regard trade unions to be enemies and continue to murder union leaders, none focus extensively on this part of the conflict. This is tragic considering the hundreds of trade unionists who have been killed in the past few years.

In terms of race and ethnicity, the news media do not fare much better. When the United States indicted several FARC members in early 2002 as members of an international terrorist group with ties to drug trafficking, it cited the kidnapping and murder of three North American activists in northeastern Colombia, along the oil pipeline partially owned by Occidental Petroleum. What the articles about the FARC indictments largely obscure is that the murdered activists—Ingrid Washinawatok, Terence Freitas, and Lahe'ane Gay—were in the region to protest *against* Occidental and actions threatening the native U'Wa tribe, perpetrated by both the FARC *and* the Colombian government. That the American government could make use of the deaths of these progressive human rights activists, who were working against understood U.S. economic interests, would seem to be indicative of the extent to which ethnic issues have been completely absent as a paradigm for viewing the conflict. Instead, the reader is left only with the information that three U.S. citizens were killed, prompting the government to respond accordingly. The issues relating to indigenous rights and their struggle against state-sponsored mega-projects and multinational oil exploration are not considered relevant. Indeed, none of the very few articles that even mention Occidental (only three in the sample) focus on the extent to which *all* sides in the conflict have violated the rights of indigenous people. The average reader would not know they even exist, which in a sense is consistent with the dominant culture's aims in the hemisphere for the past 510 years.

Tied to this is the issue of forced displacement caused by the conflict. Although a number of articles in the sample made mention of the issue, none made it a point to describe how the vast majority of the people being removed from their lands are either indigenous or of African descent, using the somewhat more ambiguous term of "peasants" to explain the phenomenon. That the displacement itself has potential economic motives is never raised, perhaps because to do so would entail a little bit more independent investigation on the part of journalists who have been too busy accumulating frequent flier miles on the many army helicopters that take them to see "war zones" first hand.

Ideological Anecdotes and Metaphors in Media Coverage

Along with the media's tendency to ignore the historic roots of the Colombian conflict, as well as the role class, race, and ethnicity have played in its development, throughout the sample one can find articles sprinkled with consistent narratives that I will call ideological anecdotes and metaphors. While in totality many patterns emerged in this respect, two of the most common were equating Colombia with the United States in the wake of September 11, and equating U.S. involvement in Colombia with its involvement in Vietnam.

Colombia = United States

In the months after the attacks on the World Trade Center, a number of articles appeared emphasizing the common plight of the American and Colombian people. One group of articles focused on the foreign nationals who died or lost their livelihoods in the attack. Eighteen Colombian victims died in the World Trade Center.[18]

A number of other articles focused on the commonalities between the lived experiences of American bystanders in the "war on terror" and those of Colombians. Typically, these articles contain a notion of America becoming a member of a global club of nations victimized by terror. A September 24 article in the *New York Times* focused on a Columbia University graduate student from Colombia, who suddenly didn't know what was safer, New York or Bogotá:

> [The] events of Sept. 11 somewhat cracked the armor Mr. Sarmiento had built around his feelings after years of witnessing violence. In the early 1990s, drug lords waged war in the streets of Bogotá. . . . his family has received letters threatening them with kidnapping. "As a Colombian and as a citizen of the world, you understand now that nowhere is safe, that any time, anywhere, anything can happen," Mr. Sarmiento said.[19]

These types of articles can be interpreted as serving a number of purposes. First, they serve to humanize victims of violence by contextualizing the human suffering in one conflict in terms that readers understand on a gut level. This is good old-fashioned feature writing and is not so much a problem. Second, and more significant in taking this approach, it is easier to present the argument that common victimhood implies a common enemy, which in turn may justify common responses and solutions. This is a reflection of the wide-angle September 11 lens many reporters are using to view the world these days. When writing about the still-unresolved anthrax attacks against a number of media organizations in the fall of 2001, reporter Felicity Barringer also fell into this model of simplistic linkages between totally unconnected events:

> Even groups who profess hatred of the media use it to raise their profile. Individual reporters are attacked and even killed—by criminal organizations in Colombia, Islamic radicals in Algeria or armed insurgents in Sierra Leone. But news company headquarters, both in the United States and around the world, are accustomed to verbal assaults, not physical ones.[20]

In this case, perhaps we can excuse the reporter for not having much else to report on that day as very little information was coming out about the "anthrax attacker." You may recall that most news media were depending on speculation and hypothetical situations to fill their coverage during that period. But to mention Colombia within the context of attacks on the media once again detaches those attacks from the political motivations behind them. To compare the relatively arbitrary anthrax incidents to years of systematic repression of independent and free expression in Colombia, very often carried out by agents of the state (or at least friendly to the state) seems to me to be an exercise in frivolity.

Colombia = Vietnam

Perhaps the most prevalent metaphor used in U.S. news media outlets is that of Vietnam. Typically, the war in Vietnam is evoked as a cautionary marker or symbol of a conflict that could be internally contentious and divisive within the United States, largely unwinnable, and difficult to pull out of once troops are committed. The case of Colombia has often been referred to as another Vietnam. A concept that arises repeatedly in the sample is the idea of "quagmire," as in Joseph Contreras's article in *Newsweek* "A Little Vietnam," where he asks "just how far is the Bush administration willing to wade into the Colombian quagmire?"[21] Or in a *Washington Post* editorial on February 24, 2002, where critics of Bush's policies are described as being afraid "that more substantial U.S. military aid will lead to a Vietnam-like quagmire."[22] The *Boston Globe* dedicated a 1,000-word article in its June 16, 2002, edition, that focused on how a number of New England lawmakers were growing increasingly impatient with the administration's policies in Colombia, quoting Representative James McGovern (D-MA) as saying, "This is Gulf of Tonkin–type of language" that is "about getting involved in a nasty civil war. It has nothing to do with terrorism."[23]

On the surface, evoking the Vietnam War, one of the least popularly supported conflicts in U.S. history, would appear to connote a broad opposition to U.S. involvement in the region, and in particular Colombia. However, the symbolism of Vietnam in this case does not appear to be meant to connote imperialism or extreme levels of suffering and death in the noncombatant population. How a direct U.S. military engagement in Colombia would affect the people in the country is never raised. Instead, it is understood in a distinctly reactionary context, almost exclusively from the perspective of the United States. That is, in terms of the domestic political and economic costs of such a war. Again, Colombia is not the only country that receives this kind of ethnocentric treatment, as sociologist Herbert Gans would describe it. One need only consider the twenty-four-hour coverage leading up to the latest war in Iraq. In this case, the potential for war was constantly being framed in a similar fashion in late 2002 and early 2003; that Iraqi civilians might die in a United States–led attack was usually an afterthought for television pundits, if mentioned at all. After the end of official combat announced by President Bush in May 2003, the body count that followed was exclusively of U.S. forces, with Iraqi losses completely erased from the public imagination.

Indeed, Vietnam is referenced more as a pragmatic policy metaphor rather than as a moral perspective. As a result, that the involvement itself is highly contentious becomes invisible. The news media's tendency to cite the Vietnam issue also ignores the long history of U.S. involvement in Colombia described in the previous chapters. The United States has trained thousands of Colombian soldiers over the last forty years, with the largest number of graduates from the U.S. Army School of the Americas coming from Colombia; U.S. advisors and trainers from a wide array of military, intelligence, and law-enforcement agencies have maintained a regular presence on the ground in Colombia for the last forty years, and in particular since the late 1980s; more than $2 billion in U.S. aid has gone there, primarily in the form of security assistance, since 1999 alone. Obviously it is not a full-scale military invasion of the kind we witnessed in Southeast Asia, but U.S. involvement in Colombia historically should not be discarded in terms of the impact it has had on the way the conflict has played out. Over the years I have tried to avoid the Vietnam analogy at all costs when it comes to Colombia for these reasons, even when discussing Colombia within progressive environments.

Coding of Terror: The Subtext of U.S. News Media Coverage

As we can see from some of the samples just mentioned, one of the primary means through which news stories are infused with broader meaning is the labeling and association of the subject with symbols and metaphors that have resonance to the readership. Within U.S. media coverage of world events in general, and Colombia specifically, one of the most important of these concepts is the idea of "terrorism."

Within the sample, a significant range of actions are deemed to fit within this term. Generally, "terror" and "terrorism" are used at face value to define violent actions, perpetrated by a nonstate group against innocent civilians. Recognizing the subjectivity of the term, many of the articles seemed to shy away from using the word *terrorism* in a nonattributed form, opting instead to attribute accusations of terror to partisans. In contrast, the term *terror* appears quite often in a nonattributed form, disproportionately labeling the FARC.

What is significant, however, is not so much how the articles superficially define the terms of terror, but how the use of this heavily loaded term influences the subtexts and broader media narrative of the war in Colombia. Outside of its descriptive power, the word *terrorism* signifies and implies a number of truisms that directly inform how newspaper articles are read.

One of the most obvious of these truisms is that it is impossible to negotiate with terrorists. This stems from the idea that terrorist groups do not operate on the same rational/materialist precepts of legitimate state structures, or that there is little potential overlap between the goals of the two parties. In this context, "terrorists" can be differentiated from "insurgents" or "rebels," who are assumed to have a minimum degree of potential interest-overlap with the government. In fact, these lines are extremely blurry and often arbitrary. Yet the ability to cast one side as terrorists serves to simultaneously undermine the validity of "rebel" grievances, while legitimating its adversaries, and their motivations.[24]

Within the sample, there is demonstrated evidence of attempts by government officials to change perceptions of the FARC from their traditional label of "Marxist rebels" or "insurgents" to terrorists and "narcoterrorists." Many articles highlight this process as much as its implications. For example, *Washington Post* reporter Karen DeYoung observes that increasing attacks by the FARC on civilians and prominent politicians have "ended any FARC claim to political legitimacy and changed their label from 'insurgents' to 'terrorists.'"[25] Focusing on then-president Andres Pastrana, DeYoung notes that he "had been reluctant to call the guerrillas terrorists as long as he was conducting peace negotiations with them."[26] However, the vast majority of the sample provides little indication of this process of changing terminology, and in so doing ultimately falls back on the "good guy"/"bad guy" binary.

On the flip side, at times news reports tend to distort the picture of who the AUC actually are, using terms such as *vigilantes* or *guerrillas* to describe them, thus deliberately taking away their terrorist tendencies. This occurred throughout the one-year monitoring period, and continued even into 2003. Such was the case with an Associated Press headline that read "Colombia Ready for Talks with Rebel Group" on January 8, 2003. This piece happens to be outside of the one-year sample but is illustrative of the double standard that exists if one considers the magnitude of what the story may have been referring to. Reading the headline, one is immediately made to assume that a major breakthrough has taken place whereby the Uribe administration was preparing to resume a dialogue with

the FARC less than six months after taking office, a development that most would have considered unfathomable. As the
reader gets into the article, however, it becomes clear that the
piece was actually about the paramilitary's hope to start up
peace talks with Uribe, and not about the FARC or the ELN,
who were nowhere near the negotiating table.[27] In this instance,
one must either redefine the term "rebel," or simply erase a
long history of collaboration between the AUC and the state
that they're supposedly rebelling against, an issue addressed in
chapter 4.

The FARC are often equated with other "terrorist" groups
like the Irish Republican Army, as well as the cocaine cartels
of the past, such as Pablo Escobar's Medellín cartel, usually
through the attributions of government officials. Asa Hutchinson, chief of the U.S. Drug Enforcement Agency, is quoted
repeatedly in Tim Weiner's February 22, 2002, article in the
New York Times. He writes: "Mr. Hutchinson said the United
States would welcome an assault on a guerrilla group, the Revolutionary Armed Forces of Colombia, whom he called "'narcoterrorists' working in league with Colombia's drug lords."[28]
Needless to say, this designation is repeated regularly throughout the sample, and continues to this day.

Again, journalists are careful in attributing the accusations
and charges made against the FARC to officials and/or experts in
order to avoid the appearance of having any particular position
on the matter. Nevertheless, what must be considered is the
overall message that an article or a series of articles sends to the
reader through the structure and tone of the piece(s). A May 5,
2002, article in the Sunday edition of the *Boston Globe* is an
example of how balance is not always what it's cut out to be.
Written by correspondent Bryan Bender, the 1,012-word piece
focuses on the Bush administration's accelerated push to link the
FARC "to some of the same global groups that are the target of

Washington's expanding war on international terrorism." Although Bender points out in the third paragraph that critics of Bush's strategy "say that alleged ties between Colombian guerrillas and such global terror groups as the Al Qaeda network are weak at best," the next nine paragraphs are dedicated to espousing the administration's view. He quotes Secretary of State Colin Powell's claim that "in the past year, there's a lot of fertilization taking place between different terrorist organizations and, with each passing day, you can begin to see different connections emerge that have to be pursued," adding that "we have to have the flexibility it needs to go after this kind of threat" in Colombia. This statement is the clearest indication of how the Bush team has openly rewritten the history of Colombia's guerrilla movement, with little challenge from a supposedly informed journalist. In fact, following Powell's quote, Bender goes on to quote the Republican staff of the House International Relations Committee "alleging connections between the FARC and various international terrorist organizations and supporters, including the Irish Republican Army, Iranian agents, the Lebanese Hezbollah, and Al Qaeda"; Deputy Secretary of State Richard Armitage, who testified before the House Appropriations Committee that "Al Qaeda supporters have been active in the tri-border area of Colombia, Peru, and Ecuador"; and Attorney General John Ashcroft, who called FARC "a fiercely anti-American terrorist organization." This statement is followed by the resident analyst, in other words the one person who could be expected to have a neutral voice on the issue, Alberto Alesina, "a Colombia expert at Harvard University," who said: "It is certainly clear that there is nobody willingly supporting the FARC other than terrorists and militants. . . . The view of the left that these people are some sort of freedom fighters is totally misguided. Like terrorists, they have no interest in negotiating. The change in policy is to eliminate them militarily."[29]

To oppose the onslaught of the FARC–equals–Al Qaeda allegations, toward the end of the article Bender finally presents the voice of Massachusetts congressman William Delahunt, who called the claims "an effort to secure more involvement and military assistance to Colombia." Bender also quotes an unidentified intelligence official who said in a typically American way "It's a very lawless, Old West-type of place and every type of bad person operates there," but to equate the FARC with Hezbollah or Al Qaeda, well, "the experts just laugh." Finally, in the second-to-last line Bender writes: "A recent report published by the Council on Foreign Relations said "there is no evidence linking the Islamists of Al Qaeda to the FARC or *two right-wing paramilitary groups* in Colombia, the National Liberation Army, and the United Self-Defense Forces of Colombia" (emphasis added).[30] Here two things stand out. First, Bender betrays his limited knowledge of the situation in Colombia by referring to the ELN as a "right-wing paramilitary group." But more important, even if we were to accept the gaffe as an honest mistake, it is the only mention in the entire piece of the AUC and its potential links to international terrorist organizations. Yes, the source discounts FARC–Al Qaeda links, but only after an entire article building such suspicions in the reader's mind. Meanwhile, officials immediately erased any suspicions of the AUC's ties to Islamic terrorists.

This idea of "terrorism" implicitly exempts major contingents within the war of a role in the atrocities of the conflict, most notably the Colombian government. Defining the acts of violence in the war as terrorism locates the origins of violence away from the government. This is most clearly evidenced in the prevalent narrative/"truism" that massacres and other acts of terror are perpetrated primarily by the FARC and to a lesser extent by the paramilitaries, most notably the AUC. The flip side of this narrative is the assumption that the Colombian and

American governments/militaries are not actively colluding in paramilitary actions.

This idea is constantly enforced by the presentation of the conflict as a multifront battle between the legitimate democratic government of Colombia versus all other factions. In a *Washington Post* editorial, for example, the paper portrays the situation as "Colombia's battle with insurgent groups of the left and right," with the Colombian government locked in a "fight against extremists who routinely use terrorism to weaken a democratic and pro-American government."[31]

The concept of terrorism, as used in this editorial and in much of the sample, sets up a relational binary equation in which the perpetrators of terror are given parity. Thus, the FARC and AUC are presented as equal, in terms (1) of their violent actions, and (2) in terms of their relation to the government, that is, both are equal enemies. Due to the prevalence of this relational idea, it becomes possible to reduce the conflict into a simplistic and ultimately flawed narrative of "bad guys [paramilitaries], killing other bad guys [leftist guerrillas]."[32]

This parity is extremely problematic for a number of reasons. First, it further decontextualizes and obscures the sides of the conflict and the sources of their grievances. This speaks to the problem of lack of origins/history elaborated above. Second, it distorts the differences in the substantive initiative and acts of violence and intimidation employed by the FARC and AUC. In Peter Romero's *Washington Post* op-ed piece, he makes the highly deceptive yet true observation that "over 90 percent of . . . offenses (human rights abuses and extrajudicial deaths) are committed by guerrillas and paramilitaries."[33] If we were to accept the idea of parity between the paramilitaries and the FARC, we would expect that, of this 90 percent of abuses, they were split roughly evenly (meaning that 45 percent of abuses were committed by each side). Yet as has already been pointed out, 70–75 percent of human rights violations in Colombia are attributable to the AUC. The portrayal of terrorist "parity" in the U.S. media may be the result of foreign journalists being indirectly influenced by the way their Colombian counterparts report on the conflict. In the Colombian news media, it is not even a question of parity anymore but rather a consistent presentation of the FARC as being the most violent of the illegal groups, while the paramilitaries are seen as more acceptable. This tendency is reflected in the starkly different treatment the Colombian news media gave to the peace talks between the FARC and the government and the current process between the AUC and the government.

An equally flawed consequence of this portrayal of the conflict is that it renders the Colombian and U.S. governments effectively invisible in the excesses of the conflict. Indeed, while many articles make passing references to the collusion between the Colombian government and paramilitaries, none proceed to the implication that the government itself is at least partially directly responsible for the excesses committed in the name of fighting the rebels. Similarly, none of the articles explores the possibility of U.S. complicity in these actions, despite the government's acknowledged presence in the country.

The U.S. invisibility in this equation is further accentuated by repetitive references to "new ways of thinking" ushered in by September 11. Once again, perhaps most explicit in this regard is Bryan Bender's *Boston Globe* report on January 17, 2002, in which he writes: "Closer to home, the Bush Administration is discussing plans to expand U.S. military involvement in Colombia's civil war," going on to quote Secretary of Defense Donald Rumsfeld, who said "We are interested in a lot more than Al Qaeda. For it to have our interest . . . a terrorist network . . . need not have been directly connected to September 11."[34] This picture may create the false impression that there hasn't been too much U.S. involvement in the conflict before, thus erasing the last fifteen years or so of intensive training, arms shipments, and other military assistance in the name of the war on drugs, not to mention the previous forty years of involvement. Furthermore, by failing to mention that one of the "terrorist" groups operating in Colombia has been working closely with Washington's principal ally in the region—the Colombian army—since their inception in the mid-1980s, Bender commits a pretty serious oversight in reporting "the facts."

This narrative is difficult to sustain, given the significant degree of evidence to the contrary. Thus, many articles shy away from directly painting these relations, instead tending to employ a softer amended narrative, which tends to isolate this collusion to fringe components of the military, while keeping actual details of massacres on the ground to a minimum. Yet even within this murkier context, a number of interesting and important equations and implicit arguments emerge that serve to infuse the conflict with decontextualized ideological significance, further distorting the picture for the news consumer. Perhaps the most consistent implication that comes up again and again is that the United States is concerned about human rights, about fortifying the Colombian state in order to weed out the bad apples, and that the Colombian government is dedicated to the same principles. The myths of Colombian democracy mentioned in chapter 1 are thereby perpetuated even further.

Media Coverage and Its Impact on Policy

In truth, this brief analysis only scratches the surface and does not begin to tackle the more complex questions relating to what impact this type of short-sighted news media coverage may actually have on the unfolding situation on the ground or on how U.S. policy vis-à-vis Colombia is shaped in Washington. One could assume that, given the tendency of the U.S. public to be generally inward looking, even if a more accurate portrayal of Colombia's sociopolitical and human rights crisis were presented in the media, there is no guarantee that it would lead the public to act to force change in that situation. As sociologist Herbert Gans correctly points out, the "media can neither produce a single and homogenous audience nor create a single effect on people."[35] In fact, it is a safe bet that Colombia would land very low on the priority list of the U.S. news consumer.

Precisely because of this, I believe it would be premature to argue that the news coverage as a whole is responsible for the way U.S. policy has evolved on the issue, or the way the human rights crisis has escalated in recent years. The human rights restrictions placed on U.S. military aid in the 1990s, for example, was less a product of accurate, responsible, and comprehensive media coverage, and more the fruit of years of activism and lobbying on the part of specific groups in the United States and Colombia to call the Colombian government to task on these issues. Clearly, groups like Human Rights Watch, Amnesty International, the Washington Office on Latin America, and the many other local and national organizations doing work on United States–Colombia policy have utilized the news media to get their positions across to the broader public. Yet this media activism was carried out with the understanding that there is never a guarantee that their positions would reach the people that mattered most: the policymakers. In any event, trying to accurately place a connection between media coverage and impact would require a whole other set of questions that I'm not convinced can be so easily answered.

Although the bulk of my analysis is based on media coverage of Colombia in the one-year period after September 11, 2001, it is clear that most of these patterns have continued since then, and they were also reflected in reports prior to the attacks on the Pentagon and the World Trade Center. In the eyes of the U.S.

news media, government policymakers, and the public in general, Colombia is first and foremost a security concern for the United States, where a democratic ally is under siege from drug-trafficking terrorists that for years have waged war against institutions of the state. In 2003, as U.S. officials applauded the hard-line measures of President Uribe, news media coverage reflected the "positive" changes being made, which in essence, as I've tried to convey in these pages, amounts to more of the same remedies applied in the past twenty years.

Again, there are exceptions to the patterns described here. Over the years I've read very good pieces by journalists covering Colombia in the *Washington Post*, the *Houston Chronicle*, the *Los Angeles Times*, *Reuters*, and elsewhere, many of them written by personal friends and people whom I regard in high esteem. On television, solid reports about Colombia have been few and far between, with the overwhelming majority focusing on the highly visual guns and bombs of the drug war, with the accompanying gross oversimplifications in language choice and historical analysis. But again, there have been some exceptions over the years in network television, the cable news channels, and PBS. Independent documentaries like the one produced by Daniel Bland, for example, have been circulated widely and clearly serve as an important counterbalance to the prevailing messages coming out of the corporate media.

Clearly, one can safely argue that the U.S. public is not adequately informed about the conflict in Colombia. Of course, this could be said about the public's understanding of Afghanistan, Iraq, the Koreas, even Canada and Mexico, our closest neighbors. Countless books have been written about the shortcomings in U.S.-style journalism that allows it to be so industrious on the one hand but so profoundly short-sighted and ethnocentric on the other. Certainly, the U.S. news consumer, overwhelmed with stories about weapons of mass destruction, terrorism, and the "valiant" efforts under-way to combat them, cannot be blamed for not having a good sense of what's at stake in Colombia and the United States' growing involvement therein. At the same time, as taxpayers funding a considerable portion of the war in Colombia, and as principal consumers of the illicit substances that this war was supposed to be preventing, their ignorance and indiffer-ence must be held accountable.

It should be pointed out that the same criticisms levied against the U.S. news media could be said about the journalism practiced elsewhere, including in Colombia itself. Indeed, the political and economic pressures that exist within U.S. corporate news organizations that lead to the type of coverage described above can be multiplied tenfold when applied to Colombian institutions of journalism. While the Colombian public is by no means removed from what is happening in the country and are forced to live with the insecurity, instability, and fear that is part and parcel of the decades-long conflict, the major corporate media in Colombia are guilty of doing a great disservice to the truth by overwhelmingly focusing on certain aspects of the conflict.[36] As one television journalist remarked recently at a public forum in Bogotá about censorship and democracy, "when it comes to ques-tions relating to security and military conflict, just about every-thing that the government says is untrue." This could be the subject of another book entirely.

Suffice it to say that as a result of this negligent news media coverage, the people of the U.S. are left in the dark about Colombia. They have been encouraged to accept an oversim-plified view of the conflict, leading to the perpetuation of the myths I described in chapter 1—myths relating to the nature of Colombian democracy, the origins of the internal conflict, and the kinds of remedies needed to resolve this conflict. In Colom-bia, the media are also guilty of perpetuating some of the same myths, with a good percentage of the population accepting them at face value. Government officials in both countries have capitalized on this. Their close relationship with the powerful media industries facilitate the process of consolidation and control. Truly dissenting perspectives are systematically marginalized.

Meanwhile, a broad cross-section of Colombian society remains shut out of the equation altogether because of the tendency of Colombian and U.S. journalists to go where the official sources take them, to point their cameras and microphones where all the noise is being generated. As a result, the many other faces of Colombia are unseen, their stories untold. I refer to the peaceful opposition, the popular social movements, human rights workers, community media activists, poets, artists, academics, and youth. These are the individuals who have not bought into the traditional narrative duplicated countless times in the daily newspapers, TV newscasts, and radio talk shows. They are the millions of people struggling through legal means for true peace with social justice in Colombia. Each day it seems as if the few spaces they have to convey their perspectives within Colombia are being reduced by the violence carried out daily by armed groups, not to mention by the intolerance of a political culture that is becoming increasingly militaristic. In the United States, not surprisingly, these voices remain invisible. It is my contention that they urgently need to be heard.

7

Conclusion:
Two Possible Futures

The dismal scenario painted in the preceding chapters may leave the impression that there is little hope for change, that the only viable option is to surrender the future to the warmongers and political opportunists that at any given moment seem to have the upper hand. Considering the deep-rooted divisions that have always existed in Colombia and the historical tendency to resolve those differences through the use of violence, it is not an unreasonable conclusion to make, however disheartening it may be.

This universal pessimism is nurtured by the current global climate, especially since September 11, 2001. Military confrontation has become the primary means to address real and perceived threats, in turn fueling further radicalization and polarization. The seeds of those threats, be they economic and social marginalization or cultural annihilation, are rarely addressed. Making matters worse, the divisions between the haves and the have-nots continue to widen at the same time that economic policies developed and promoted in the powerful institutions based in the global north take effect with little to no opposition from local governing elites in the countries of the south. Colombia may not be the only country that fits into this complex contemporary framework, although in many ways, as I hope to have made clear in these pages, it serves as a stunning case study.

Notwithstanding all of this, I remain optimistic, primarily because of my profound belief in the resilience of the Colombian people, most of whom have not given up hope for a better future. Colombia is a country of more than 44 million people— the vast majority of whom have absolutely nothing to do with either narcotrafficking or the violence whose images are so often exported for external consumption. It is true that as the conflict has escalated, society has become more polarized. But in this process, the popular social movements and peace organizations have stepped up their work toward constructing a conscious, participatory citizenry as a way of confronting years of violence, political intolerance, and exclusion. As usual, there is an ongoing and consistent effort to isolate, marginalize, and silence these groups by powerful sectors of the political establishment, especially in the current juncture. President Alvaro Uribe's "democratic security" strategy provides very little space for truly oppositional views, especially when it comes to ways of strengthening democracy. Not surprisingly, the bellicose strategies of the right-wing paramilitaries and the left-wing guerrillas also provide the popular movement with very little wiggle room.

It would be a conceptual challenge to identify the popular social movement in Colombia as one homogeneous entity or body. Numerous books have been written about the origins, goals, and long-term significance of this movement (or movements).[1] Without going into too much detail, I will take the risk of giving this movement some general characteristics. These "popular social movements" are the part of Colombian society that has traditionally been marginalized and not represented by Colombia's restrictive democracy: workers, peasants, poor women, racial and ethnic minorities such as Afro-

Colombians and indigenous people, environmentalists, and students. Locally, regionally, and on a national level, hundreds of groups have emerged in the last forty years representing diverse constituencies and using distinct tactics in achieving their objectives, from the various trade union confederations to the diverse actors in the indigenous movement, from local civic organizations to the national and local peasant associations.

Although traditionally considered to be apart from the social movement, I would also include human rights organizations in this broader framework of civil resistance, especially within the current context. Like the social movement, human rights groups have experienced differences in perspectives and approaches to the fundamental problems facing Colombia. But their common struggle to defend the fundamental rights of the population and hold the government accountable for violating those rights has made them natural allies of the popular movement, and victims in the dirty war that I described in chapter 4.

Together with confronting the state's economic development, counterdrug, and security policies, these groups, independently and in alliance with other sectors, have been presenting concrete alternatives for social, political, and economic transformation. In different parts of the country they have established territories of "peace" whereby open, public rejection of militarism is strategically promoted within the community. By taking a profoundly anti-war stance, a growing web of regional and national coalitions in defense of human rights and the search for peace with true social justice has been emerging in recent years.

There remain considerable differences, and at times particular ethnic, economic, and political interests diverge—not surprising, considering the diversity of the sectors involved. However, there is a growing sense throughout Colombia that true socioeconomic transformation can come about only with the successful convergence of these diverse constituencies, at once forced to confront the accelerated strength of the extreme right on the one hand and the increasing militarism of the armed insurgency on the other. It is safe to argue that the gradual convergence of the popular movement got underway before 1991 during the buildup toward the Constituent Assembly. But there is no doubt that it picked up considerable momentum in 1999—at about the moment that *Plan Colombia* was introduced to Colombians as the latest stage of U.S. intervention in the conflict. It was roughly at this point that people consistently began to characterize the Colombian conflict not only as a domestic struggle for economic and social justice, but also as one with profound global implications. Today, the social movement convergence is evident in five general points in which popular sectors have begun to develop a common ground where in the past one never existed:

1. Resisting globalization
2. Denouncing the state's role in paramilitarism
3. Decreasing parochialism
4. Increasing autonomy
5. Committing to a negotiated solution to the armed conflict

Because popular sectors recognize that the roots of Colombia's conflict lie in the profound economic disparities that have always existed in the country, they point to the phenomenon of globalization as one of the major reasons why the conflict has deteriorated to such a level in the past ten to fifteen years. I described some of this in chapter 5. The so-called structural reforms, the opening up of the economy, and the servicing of the debt are all manifestations of this phenomenon, with the end result being 67 percent of the population living below the poverty line in 2003. Therefore, across the board, today's popular social movements have focused their attention on resisting globalization, recognizing its negative ramifications for popular sectors throughout the country. To these sectors, the globalization of the Colombian economy has been backed up by increased military intervention from the United States, with *Plan Colombia* being the most extreme example. Now, as the Uribe administration hammers out bilateral and multilateral free-trade accords with Washington, the major unions and peasant organizations are insisting that they be included in the discussions, so as not to be once again bypassed in the interest of multinational corporate profits. Will this process result in even further economic distress for Colombian workers and peasants? If so, how will it affect the nature of the armed conflict? These are fundamental questions being raised by the popular movement as the conflict has intensified.

A second position unifying the popular social movements in Colombia is the universal recognition of the state's direct complicity in the paramilitary experiment as a tool designed to stifle widespread resistance, while systematically removing masses of people from large swaths of the national territory deemed to be of strategic and economic importance. This isn't a position that the social movements needed to be convinced of because they have lived it for the past twenty years. The primary victims of paramilitary terror between 1975 and 2000 were members of social movements or independent political organizations, both reformists and radicals, accused of being sympathizers of the guerrillas.[2] The displacement phenomenon also speaks for itself, and although the guerrillas must take some of the credit for this as well, the vast majority of the displacements can be attributed to the paramilitaries. Nevertheless, the popular social movements and the human rights community have been quite outspoken about their concerns regarding the state's complicity with paramilitaries, and they are extremely concerned about the possibility that the impending demobilization of the Autodefensas Unidas de Colombia (AUC) might turn into a process of impunity, as I outlined in chapter 4. Human rights organizations in particular are working to remind people that peace is not solely an end to the violence, but that justice must be an integral part of it. To further illustrate the level of intolerance that is part of Colombia's political system, however, these organizations continue to be branded by top government and military officials as being *voceros de la subversión*, or spokespersons for subversion, thereby keeping them permanently on the hit list of paramilitary terror, notwithstanding their independence from and consistent criticism of the guerrillas.

For example, Brigadier General José Arturo Camelo, executive director of the Defense Ministry's Judge Advocate General's office, accused human rights nongovernmental organizations (NGOs) of waging a "legal war" against the military, claiming that human rights groups were "friends of subversives" forming part of a larger strategy coordinated by the guerrillas. Furthermore, the Colombian ambassador to Portugal, Plinio Apuleyo Mendoza, after accepting his appointment to Lisbon, published a troubling column on November 24, 2002, in *El Espectador* where he linked Human Rights Watch, its executive director José Miguel Vivanco, and their colleagues in Colombia with aiding the guerrillas' cause:

> The attorneys of the Human Rights Unit have found a kindred spirit in the Chilean Marxist José Miguel Vivanco, director of Human Rights Watch . . . In Vivanco's case, one understands this phobia since, as an adolescent, [Vivanco] must have been marked forever by the gross excesses of General Pinochet and his brothers in arms. Driven by a private vindictive fervor,

he has extended that fear to the Colombian military. This has resulted in the prosecution of the best officers in the military, to the delight of Tirofijo and Mono Jojoy [a senior FARC commander].[3]

In addition, in a published interview with *El Tiempo*, Pedro Juan Moreno Villa, widely identified as a trusted Uribe advisor on security and intelligence matters who also served as vice governor during Uribe's term as governor of Antióquia, referred to NGOs as "the ones who have trashed this country. Many are leftists. The subversives and violent create these mechanisms to seize power."[4]

Defenders of Uribe were quick to argue that these off-the-cuff comments by former and present associates did not reflect the thinking of the president, and that he was indeed committed to human rights and democracy. But in September 2003, Uribe himself betrayed how he really felt about the human rights community in Colombia. After a group of eighty nongovernmental human rights groups issued a report titled "The Authoritarian Curse"[5] that was critical of some of the government's security measures, the president lashed out at them, calling human rights groups, among other things, "spokesmen for terrorism" and "politickers of terrorism." In a speech before the military's top brass, Uribe challenged human rights groups to "take off their masks . . . and drop this cowardice of hiding their ideas behind human rights."[6] If this is the kind of society Uribe wants to build in Colombia with his strategy of "democratic security," why would anybody with a true commitment to democracy want to embrace it?

A third characteristic of today's popular social movements is what I would describe as a gradual decrease in the parochialism that infested it in the past. This has led to a recognition of common areas of concern and struggle that in the past was very difficult to achieve given the many differences that existed among the distinct sectors. Although somewhat optimistic, this could be seen as a genuine attempt to construct a broad-based social movement that joins labor, indigenous people, peasants, Afro-Colombians, the displaced, and the peace and human rights movement into a viable "third way." There are several regional and national examples of this process, and it will be interesting to see how it unfolds under the Uribe government.

One issue that had kept the popular social movements from successfully joining forces in the past was the question of how to approach the armed insurgency. In other words, as popular organizations operating under legal structures, what would their public position be toward illegal opposition such as the FARC and ELN? Would alliances be built or would they distance themselves from the rebels? In almost every sector of Colombia's popular movement, this issue was the subject of major debate and tension over the years. Today, it has become less problematic, as autonomy has become a guiding principle in just about every sector, pointing to an independence of and a resistance to both the state and government forces, as well as the armed insurgency. Several factors are behind this shift, perhaps the most significant being the guerrillas' own isolation in terms of abandoning a comprehensive political strategy, opting instead for a military approach to address their grievances.

Finally, and most important, the popular social movements today have expressed an uncompromising and profound commitment to a negotiated solution to the military conflict in Colombia. Recognizing the deep social divisions that continue to exist, these groups are rightfully convinced that the first step to resolving the myriad problems facing Colombia is to begin serious, comprehensive negotiations, a dialogue with broad, inclusive, public participation, all leading to national reconciliation, reconstruction, and social justice. These groups are convinced that the FARC cannot be defeated, notwithstanding the optimistic pronouncements by the armed forces' high command. A fortification of the machine will only lead to more war, so peace talks must therefore be a policy of the state. However, the militarist policies of the Uribe administration are completely counter to this belief. That President Uribe is being encouraged and indeed fortified by the United States makes it that much more difficult for alternative positions to be heard. And because of the utter failure of the last round of peace talks with the FARC, many Colombians believe there is no need to go down that road once again. The popular movement, however, says that dialogue is the only option. Their demands are directed at not only the government but also the leadership of the guerrillas as well, who are perceived by many as not being interested in dialogue. In essence, the popular movement is trying to build a democratic, national consensus to confront all the armed actors, but also to turn back the aggressive militarist and repressive structures being put in place by Uribe.

Together and independently, these groups represent the best hope for the future of Colombia. Their struggle and their dreams are shared by tens of thousands of writers, poets, artists, students, media activists, church leaders, and intellectuals throughout the country. The Colombian people have lived through many years of civil conflict. Millions of lives have been destroyed, families divided, communities displaced. No one has been left unscathed by the bloodshed. But for years, too often the popular sectors described here have been the most victimized by terrorism, state-sponsored and otherwise. Almost daily, they have been forced to bury colleagues and loved ones who were cut down by this war. Countless others have been forced to flee the country, handcuffed by tremendous distances yet committed to struggle from afar for a better Colombia.

In the last few years, hundreds of mass actions have been carried out and pronouncements have been made public that clearly articulate these beliefs. I was moved by one that was issued in July 2003 at the XIII International Forum of Poetry and Peace for Colombia, held in Medellín. Signed by some of the most important contemporary writers in Colombia, including Juan Manuel Roca, Samuel Jaramillo, William Ospina, and Arturo Alape, its final two stanzas read:

> Colombia has before it two possible futures. We have come to comprehend how great is the abyss that divides one future that promises more atrocities in a war without end, and another that will open the way for a political negotiation with social justice.
>
> War is the arrogance in the lips of the powerful, but it is blood and misery in the humble towns and neighborhoods without hope. And after all it is the Colombian people on which the future of the nation finally depends.[7]

People in the United States have a responsibility to understand this, both as taxpayers funding a tremendous portion of the ongoing bloodshed and as consumers of the product that the U.S. government has been supposedly trying to curtail. In the accelerated process of militarization and intervention, whether in the name of the war on drugs, the war on terrorism, or the promotion of economic opportunities for U.S. transnationals, the primary casualties continue to be democracy, respect for human rights, and social justice.

And without these things, there can never be true peace in Colombia. And we'll be bound to repeat history . . . once again.

Notes

All translations of Spanish-language sources were done by the author, unless otherwise noted.

Introduction

1. See *War on Drugs Meets the War on Terror: The United States' Military Involvement in Colombia Climbs to the Next Level* (Washington, DC: Center for International Policy, February 2003).

2. DeYoung, K., & Allen, M., "Bush Shifts Strategy from Deterrence to Dominance," *The Washington Post*, September 21, 2002, p. A1.

3. Gedda, G., "House Wants Ideas to Help Colombia," Associated Press, March 7, 2002.

4. Reich, O., "La Batalla Crucial por Colombia," http://www.semana.com/, July 30, 2002, retrieved August 3, 2002.

5. See Vargas, R. *Cultivos Ilícitos y Proceso de Paz en Colombia: Una propuesta de cambio en la estrategia antidrogas hacia la solución política del conflicto* (Bogotá: Acción Andina, Transnational Institute, 2000); see also "La pobreza sigue creciendo: Uribe," *El Heraldo*, July 21, 2003, p. 8A.

6. Garcia, A., "Colombia-Estados Unidos: Alianza antidrogas," *Síntesis 2001* (Bogotá: IEPRI, Universidad Nacional, 2001), pp. 118–121.

7 Richter, P., "U.S. May Expand Aid to Colombia Policy: Powell's Remarks Come as Congress Signals Support for a Wider Role," *Washington Times*, March 7, 2002.

8. How to define the guerrillas of the FARC and the ELN has been the subject of considerable debate in recent years within Colombia. For an extensive collection of contemporary perspectives on terrorism in Colombia, see Santos A., (ed). *Terrorismo y Seguridad* (Bogotá: Planeta/Semana, 2003).

9. Sands, D., "Aid Plan Hit from Two Sides on Hill," *Washington Times*, April 12, 2002.

10. Dunne, N., & Wilson, J., "Colombian Rebels Indicted," Reuters, March 19, 2002; Hedges, M., "Guerrillas Charged with Drug Trafficking—FARC Members Face U.S. Charges," *Houston Chronicle*, March 19, 2002; DeYoung, K., "U.S. Charges Colombian Insurgents with Drug Trafficking," *Washington Post*, March 19, 2002.

11. It should be pointed out that many factors led to the breakdown in peace talks between the government of Andres Pastrana and the FARC rebels, not least of which was the failure of the FARC to demonstrate a willingness to negotiate in good faith by carrying out a number of high-profile kidnappings and political assassinations. However, there is no question that in the end, the attacks of September 11 became a convenient rallying cry against "terrorism" that was simply applied in the context of Colombia's war. Ultimately, pressure from Washington took the wind out of the sails of the negotiations.

12. Polls in Colombia, as elsewhere, must always be taken with a certain degree of skepticism. A poll published in *El Tiempo* conducted by Invamer Gallup Colombia in July 2003 showed President Uribe to have a 70 percent favorability rating, while the image of the armed forces was seen as positive by 83 percent of those polled. The catch is who were the people responding to the poll: 1,000 residents of Bogotá, Medellín, Cali, and Barranquilla, the four largest cities in the country. Naturally, the results may have come up differently had people in more remote regions of the country been questioned. See "Con Uribe, salvo la economía, todo bien," *El Tiempo*, July 23, 2003, pp. 1–2.

Chapter 1: The Myths Behind Colombian Democracy

1. As quoted in Pearce, J., *Colombia: Inside the Labyrinth* (London: Monthly Review Press/Latin America Bureau, 1990), p. 185.

2. Human Rights Watch, *State of War: Political Violence and Counterinsurgency in Colombia* (New York: Human Rights Watch, 1993), pp. 16–29.

3. Human Rights Watch. *War Without Quarter: Colombia and International Humanitarian Law* (New York: Human Rights Watch, 1998), p. 18. The Colombian Commission of Jurists reported that from July 2002 to July 2003, 6,978 people were murdered or disappeared for political reasons, while the numbers were 7,426 and 6,621 for the same period ending in 2002 and 2001, respectively. See Vargas, V. M., "Hoy, día D en apoyo de UE al gobierno de Uribe," *El Tiempo*, July 10, 2003, pp. 1–2.

4. The election of President Alvaro Uribe Vélez in May 2002 brought an end to the dual-party domination, at least on the surface. Uribe campaigned in 2001–2002 on a platform of being a break from the traditional political parties, and he is often described as a "dissident Liberal," compared at times to the populist presidential candidates of the past, such as Jorge Eliécer Gaitán,

whose assassination in 1948 sparked riots that exacerbated "La Violencia," and Luis Carlos Galán, who was killed while campaigning for president in 1989. Nevertheless, Uribe's deep connections with the Colombian political, economic, and military power structure negate his claim to being truly independent. Indeed, as far back as 1996, Uribe was considered by top officials in the Liberal establishment as presidential material; they based their support for him on what they considered to be the successful "Uribe Model" of civilian self-defense groups that he had established in the department of Antióquia when he was governor. These *Asociaciones Comunitarias de Seguridad*, or Community Security Associations, were criticized by human rights groups, including Amnesty International, as being a violation of international humanitarian law because they made civilians both potential victims and victimizers in the military conflict. This model, which was given the term "Convivir," is the basis of Uribe's strategy of creating a 1 million person "civilian patrol" to assist the armed forces in its "counterterrorism" war. In short, it's fair to say that his election was not a break from the Liberal-Conservative stronghold. Indeed, he was endorsed by the Conservative Party. And prior to Uribe's inauguration, this "candidate for change" was warmly embraced by major national and international business players who were clearly comfortable that he was a person who would create a climate favorable to their interests. See Wilson, S., "Colombian Candidate Runs Mostly Out of Sight—Threats on His Life by Rebels Kept Front-runner's Campaign Off the Streets and on the Screen," *Washington Post*, May 21, 2002; Carrigan, A., "War or Peace? Colombia's New President Must Choose Between Washington and His Own People," *In These Times*, August 2002; "Mano dura o tenaza paramilitar? Por que en Antióquia el modelo predicado por Uribe Vélez no es tan bueno como lo pintan?", *Alternativa*, December 1996, No. 5; *El Tiempo*, "Multinacionales respaldan al gobierno de Alvaro Uribe," July 23, 2002.

5. Bushnell, D., *The Making of Modern Colombia: A Nation in Spite of Itself* (Berkeley: University of California Press, 2001), p. 285.

6. Giraldo, J. *Colombia: Genocidal Democracy* (Monroe, ME: Common Courage Press, 1996), p. 57.

7. Molano, A., "Violence and Land Colonization," in *Violence in Colombia: The Contemporary Crisis in Historical Perspective*. Ed. C. Berquist, R. Peñaranda, and G. Sánchez (Wilmington, DE: Scholarly Resources Books, 1992), p. 195.

8. In the 1980s, for example, Colombia was the only country in all of Latin America that did not experience a negative rate of growth at any time during the decade. Some observers attribute the relative economic stability in Colombia to the political power sharing between the two parties, where fiscal policy has remained more or less consistent over the years, thereby avoiding any sudden jolts in macroeconomic terms, (see Bushnell, *The Making of Modern Colombia*, pp. 268–277). Others have pointed to the tremen-

dous amounts of money generated through the illicit drug trade over the years as a reason for the relative stability of Colombia's economy, although this has been discounted by more thorough analyses. For a good review of the most recent literature about Colombia's dependence on drug money and its impact on the national economy, see Reina, M., "Drug Trafficking and the National Economy," in *Violence in Colombia, 1990-2000: Waging War and Negotiating Peace*, Ed. C. Berquist, R. Peñaranda, and G. Sánchez (Wilmington, DE: Scholarly Resources Books, 2001), pp. 75–94. In this essay, Reina discounts the so-called positive benefits the drug trade has provided for Colombia's economy, and points to a number of ways in which it has actually been detrimental to overall growth.

9. Arcieri, V., "Pobreza devora a Cartagena," *El Tiempo*, July 30, 2003, p. 6.

10. See Wade, P., *Blackness and Race Mixture: The Dynamics of Racial Identity in Colombia* (Baltimore: Johns Hopkins University Press, 1993), pp. 3–47.

11. The numbers vary considerably. For example, Piedad Córdoba, in "Las comunidades negras frente al conflicto interno y los procesos de paz en Colombia," September 25, 1999, says the black population is 20 percent; Juan de Dios Mosquera Mosquera, in *Las Comunidades Negras de Colombia Hacia el Siglo XXI* (Bogotá: Docentes Editores, 2000), says the population is 45 percent black, based on the breakdown of the population into three distinct sectors: "Africanos criollos," which represent the community that has maintained the pure blood African, mostly in the Pacific region and in the islands of San Andres, Providencia and Santa Catalina; "Afroindígenas," the population of mixed black and Indian blood, who live in the Atlantic plains, and in the valleys of the Rivers Cauca and Magdalena; and "Afromestizos," a mixture of black and the mestizo population of Indo-Hispanics that identify themselves as white, were formerly identified as mulattoes by the Spanish, and populate large urban areas.

12. Depto. Nacional de Planeación, DNP, "Plan Nacional de Desarrollo de la población Afrocolombiana, 1999," in *Racismo y Discriminación Racial en Colombia* (Bogotá: Cimarrón, 2000).

13. Waisbord, S., "Grandes Gigantes: Media Concentration in Latin America," www.opendemocracy.net, February 27, 2002; retrieved June 11, 2002.

14. See Giraldo, *Colombia: Genocidal Democracy*, p. 59; also, López de la Roche describes how trade unionists have been depicted over the years by the Colombian media, in Archila, M., and Pardo, M., eds., *Movimientos sociales, estado y democrácia en Colombia* (Bogotá: Centro de Estudios Sociales, Universidad Nacional de Colombia, 2001), pp. 483–488.

15. Waisbord, S., *Watchdog Journalism in South America, News Accountability and Democracy* (New York: Columbia University Press, 2001), p. 17.

Chapter 2: Colombia's Un-Civil Conflict

1. Alape, A., *La paz, la violencia: Testigos de excepción*, 6th edition. (Bogotá: Planeta, 1997), p. 20.

2. Ibid., p. 23.

3. Sánchez, G., "The Violence: An Interpretive Synthesis," in *Violence in Colombia: The Contemporary Crisis in Historical Perspective*, Ed. C. Berquist, R. Peñaranda, and G. Sánchez (Wilmington, DE: Scholarly Resources Books, 1992), p. 77.

4. Ibid., p. 78.

5. There has been widespread speculation that the murder of Gaitán was carried out under the orders of the U.S. CIA. For years, demands have been made by a growing movement within Colombia to declassify U.S. intelligence documents surrounding the murder of Gaitán. See *Saqueo de una Ilusión: El 9 de Abril—50 años después* (Bogotá: Número Ediciones, 1998). See also Sánchez, G. *Grandes Potencias, el 9 de Abril y la Violencia* (Bogotá: Planeta Editorial, 2000).

6. Sánchez, G., "The Violence: An Interpretive Synthesis," in *Violence in Colombia: The Contemporary Crisis in Historical Perspective*, Ed. C. Berquist, R. Peñaranda, and G. Sánchez (Wilmington, DE: Scholarly Resources Books, 1992), p. 77.

7. For a number of interesting reflections on the period of *El Bogotazo*, see *Saqueo de una Ilusión: El 9 de Abril—50 años después* (Bogotá: Número Ediciones, 1998). Countless other books in both Spanish and English have been written about this period, a list too large to mention here.

8. Sánchez, G. (1992), p. 90.

9. Ibid., pp. 103–104.

10. Ibid., p. 112.

Chapter 3: The Contemporary Guerrilla Movement

1. For a compact yet comprehensive look at the guerrilla movements, see Pizarro, E., "Revolutionary Guerrilla Groups in Colombia," in *Violence in Colombia: The Contemporary Crisis in Historical Perspective*, Ed. C. Berquist, R. Peñaranda, and G. Sánchez (Wilmington, DE: Scholarly Resources Books, 1992), pp. 169–193; also, for a detailed analysis in Spanish of the various political leftist tendencies in Colombia, see Sánchez, R. *Crítica y Alternativa: Las Izquierdas en Colombia* (Bogotá: Ediciones la Rosa Roja, 2001).

2. From "Programa Agrario de los Guerrilleros," published in Jacobo Arenas, *Diario de la Resistencia de Marquetalia* (Bogotá: Ediciones Abejón Mono, 1973), p. 130.

3. See, for example, Ramsey, R. W., *Guerrilleros y Soldados* (Bogotá: Editorial Tercer Mundo, 1981); see also Sánchez, G. and Meertens, D., *Bandits, Peasants and Politics: The Case of "La Violencia" in Colombia* (Austin: University of Texas Press, 2001).

4. Alape, A., *Tirofijo: Los Sueños y las Montañas*, 4th edition (Bogotá: Planeta Editorial, 1998).

5. For an excellent account of the events of the Palace of Justice attack and its impact on the M-19, the guerrilla movement in general, and Colombia's contemporary human rights crisis, see Carrigan, A., *The Palace of Justice: A Colombian Tragedy* (New York: Four Walls Eight Windows, 1993).

6. Many other guerrilla groups have emerged since the 1960s, with varying degrees of impact and relevance. The most notable is the indigenous group Armed Movement Quintín Lame (MQL), named after the Páez Indian leader who led the fight for the recuperation of indigenous territory in the departments of Cauca and Tolima in the 1920s and 1930s. The MQL was more of an armed self-defense force that accompanied the process of land invasions being carried out by indigenous communities in the 1970s and 1980s. The violent backlash against the indigenous leadership spearheaded by the armed forces under the auspices of large landowners led to the creation of the group. In some instances, they forged alliances with the M-19 and the FARC, although they maintained their autonomy throughout the process. In 1991 they signed a peace agreement with the government, and like the M-19, participated in the Constituent Assembly that rewrote Colombia's Constitution (in total, the Constituent Assembly had three representatives from Colombia's indigenous communities, the result of years of nonviolent mobilizing by the indigenous movement and the pressure brought upon the state by the Quintín Lame).

7. Vargas Meza, R., "The Revolutionary Armed Forces of Colombia and the Illicit Drug Trade" (Washington, DC: Acción Andina/Transnational Institute/WOLA, June 1999).

8. See Bushnell, D., *The Making of Modern Colombia: A Nation in Spite of Itself* (Berkeley: University of California Press, 2001), p. 253.

9. See Vargas Meza, R., "The Revolutionary Armed Forces of Colombia and the Illicit Drug Trade."

10. "Plataforma para un gobierno de reconstrucción y reconciliación nacional," *Documento*, April 3, 1993, Octava Conferencia Nacional Guerrillera, FARC;

taken from *Corporación Observatorio para la Paz, las Verdaderas Intenciones de las FARC* (Bogotá: Intermedio Editores, 1999), pp. 32–37.

11. From "Colombia Human Rights Certification IV." Issued by Human Rights Watch, Amnesty International, WOLA, September 2002, http://hrw.org/backgrounder/americas/colombia-certification4.htm; retrieved January 14, 2003.

12. U.S. Committee for Refugees, "Americas: September 11 Led to Freeze in U.S. Refugee Admissions; Displacement Continued Unabated in Colombia," June 6, 2002, from *World Refugee Survey, 2002*.

13. "Organización Indígena de Antióquia—OIA—Violaciones a los derechos humanos e infracciones al derecho internacional humanitario" (internal document), August 2001.

14. Garcia, C., "Colombian President Under Fire for Failed Security Measures, Constitutional Referendum," Associated Press, May 19, 2003; see also "Un desafío para la política de seguridad," *El Tiempo*, July 14, 2003, p. 2.

15. Forero, J., "Shifting Colombia's Aid: U.S. Focuses on Rebels," *New York Times*, August 10, 2002.

16. Toro, J. P., "Colombia's Armed Groups on the Verge of Demise, Defense Minister Says," Associated Press, January 18, 2003.

17. Ortega Guerrero, M., "Iglesia insiste en la salida negociada," *El Tiempo*, July 3, 2003, p. 5.

18. From author interview with Raul Reyes, during the São Paulo Forum, San Salvador, El Salvador, July 1996, aired on Pacifica Radio's *Our Americas*, August 1996; excerpts from the interview were published in *NACLA Report on the Americas*, XXXI: No. 1, July/August 1997.

19. In a large exposé in the weekly magazine *Semana*, former Salvadoran guerrilla commander Joaquín Villalobos outlined a series of reasons for why the FARC was losing the war. Villalobos, J. "Por qué las FARC están perdiendo la guerra," *Semana*, July 7–14, 2003, pp. 22–28.

20. "Guerrilla desvirtúa triunfos militares," *El Heraldo*, July 15, 2003, p. 1D.

21. Selsky, A., "Debate Surrounds UN Envoy Colombia Quip," Associated Press, May 21, 2003; "Naciones Unidas dice que la interpretaron incorrectamente," *El Tiempo*, July 2, 2003, p. 4.

22. "El regaño de San José," *Cambio*, June 23, 2003, p. 29.

23. One of the ideas Uribe does support regarding the United Nations is the introduction of an international verification body, perhaps the so-called Blue Helmets, to guarantee security in the regions where the right-wing paramilitaries have agreed to demobilize. As of September 2003, this issue was far from being resolved, but it was clear that the FARC was against any international

"peace-keeping" presence. See Sierra, L. M., and Mercado, B., "A un paso de los Cascos Azules," *El Tiempo*, July 27, 2003, p. 14.

24. Sánchez, R., *Crítica y Alternativa: Las Izquierdas en Colombia* (Bogotá: Ediciones la Rosa Roja, 2001), p. 295.

25. Restrepo, L. A., "The Crisis of the Current Political Regime and Its Possible Outcomes," in V*iolence in Colombia: The Contemporary Crisis in Historical Perspective*, Ed. C. Berquist, R. Peñaranda, and G. Sánchez (Wilmington, DE: Scholarly Resources Books, 1992), p. 274.

Chapter 4: The "Paramilitaries" and the Dirty War

1. "Panorama de Derechos Humanos y Derecho Humanitario," Colombian Commission of Jurists, Bogotá, February 26, 2001. See also Vargas, V. M., "Hoy, día D en apoyo de UE al gobierno de Uribe," *El Tiempo*, July 10, 2003, p. 2.

2. The term *paramilitary* has a generic tone to it that covers a broad array of distinct forces with various historical trajectories. These forces' origins stretch back to the late 1950s during the first government of the National Front, when in southern Tolima, armed groups of anticommunists started up civic "self-defense" committees to confront the peasant rebel holdouts fighting the government. In the 1960s, these groups were given legal status as part of the government's imposed state of internal commotion. By the 1980s, they took on different formations, to which today's paramilitaries can trace their closest connections. These include paid assassins operating under the auspices of the Medellín cartel in the 1980s, private armies used to protect certain landholdings and other powerful economic interests, and army-backed "self-defense" groups that were once protected by the law and were aimed at confronting guerrilla extortion and kidnapping. These regional groups, many of which have direct ties to the national police and armed forces, merged in 1997 and became the current national umbrella organization known as the Autodefensas Unidas de Colombia (AUC), which has its origins in all of these formations. The main distinction is that the AUC has a clear political-military program directed exclusively against the guerrillas in order to gain territorial control in vital regions of strategic importance. For a systematic yet succinct historical analysis of these different formations and the contemporary paramilitaries, see Cubides, F., "From Private to Public Violence: The Paramilitaries," in *Violence in Colombia, 1990–2000: Waging War and Negotiating Peace*, Ed. C. Berquist, R. Peñaranda, and G. Sánchez (Wilmington, DE: Scholarly Resources Books, 2001), pp. 127–149; another excellent account that describes in great detail the origins and nature of the paramilitaries is Kirk, R., *More Terrible Than Death: Massacres, Drugs and America's War in Colombia* (New York: Public Affairs, 2003). In Spanish, see Romero, M., *Para-*

militares y autodefensas: 1982–2003 (Bogotá: Instituto de Estudios Políticos y Relaciones Internacionales, Universidad Nacional de Colombia, 2003). See also "¿El principio del fin de las AUC?" *El Espectador*, July 20, 2003, p. 2A.

3. Restrepo, L. A., "The Equivocal Dimensions of Human Rights in Colombia," *Violence in Colombia, 1990–2000: Waging War and Negotiating Peace*, Ed. C. Berquist, R. Peñaranda, and G. Sánchez (Wilmington, DE: Scholarly Resources Books, 2001), p. 102; Romero makes a very elaborate and meticulous case for why the paramilitaries emerged so forcefully in the 1980s, precisely during a period of relative political opening and negotiations with the guerrillas; *Paramilitares y autodefensas: 1982–2003* (Bogotá: Instituto de Estudios Políticos y Relaciones Internacionales, Universidad Nacional de Colombia, 2003), pp. 16–42. His book provides an excellent analysis of the political reasons for the expansion of the paramilitary project, namely how it was a direct attempt to derail any possible democratic opening in the countryside and government rapprochement with the leftist insurgency.

4. Human Rights Watch, *The Sixth Division: Military-Paramilitary Ties and U.S. Policy in Colombia* (New York: Human Rights Watch, 2001), p. 12.

5. U.S. Committee for Refugees (USCR), "Americas: September 11 Led to Freeze in U.S. Refugee Admissions; Displacement Continued Unabated in Colombia," June 6, 2002, from *World Refugee Survey, 2002*; see also, *War on Drugs Meets the War on Terror: The United States' Military Involvement in Colombia Climbs to the Next Level* (Washington, DC: Center for International Policy, February 2003).

6. Romero, *Paramilitares y autodefensas: 1982-2003* (Bogotá: Instituto de Estudios Políticos y Relaciones Internacionales, Universidad Nacional de Colombia, 2003), pp. 15–16.

7. Cubides, F., "From Private to Public Violence: The Paramilitaries," in *Violence in Colombia, 1990-2000: Waging War and Negotiating Peace*, Ed. C. Berquist, R. Peñaranda, and G. Sánchez (Wilmington, DE: Scholarly Resources Books, 2001), p.132, citing Reyes, A., "Conflicto armado y territorio en Colombia," in *Colonización del bosque húmedo tropical* (Bogotá: Planeta, 1989), p. 55.

8. From Corporación Colectivo de Abogados José Alvear Restrepo, *¿Terrorismo o Rebelión?* (Bogotá: Intermedio Editores, 2001), pp. 13–14.

9. U.S. Committee for Refugees (USCR), "Americas: September 11 Led to Freeze in U.S. Refugee Admissions; Displacement Continued Unabated in Colombia," June 6, 2002, from *World Refugee Survey, 2002*.

10. Paragraph 16, "Report of the UN High Commissioner for Human Rights on the Human Rights Situation in Colombia," February 8, 2001, www.unhchr.ch/ .

11. Human Rights Watch, The *Sixth Division: Military-Paramilitary Ties and U.S. Policy in Colombia* (New York: Human Rights Watch, 2001), p. 12.

12. Ibid., p. 4.

13. Colombia Nunca Más, "Los diálogos con el paramilitarismo: ¿Paz o impunidad?" *Desde Abajo*, June 15–July 15, 2003, pp. 6–8.

14. "Colombia Human Rights Certification IV," issued by Human Rights Watch, Amnesty International, WOLA, September 2002, http://hrw.org/backgrounder/americas/colombia-certification4.htm ; retrieved January 14, 2003.

15. Ibid., http://hrw.org/backgrounder/americas/colombia-certification4.htm ; the same criticisms were levied against the State Department's certification in July 2003, the fifth time in three years that Washington gave the green light to the Colombian military, despite evidence that the military was not complying with conditions stipulated in U.S. law. See Gómez Maseri, S., "E.U. certifica a Colombia," *El Tiempo*, July 9, 2003, pp. 1–5.

16. Human Rights Watch, *The Sixth Division*, p. 16, citing various sources.

17. See, for example, Wilson, S., "24 Dead but Alliance Endures: Colombian Army's Clash with Paramilitary Troops May Be an Aberration," http://www.washingtonpost.com; retrieved September 18, 2002.

18. Romero, M., *Paramilitares y autodefensas: 1982–2003* (Bogotá: Instituto de Estudios Políticos y Relaciones Internacionales, Universidad Nacional de Colombia, 2003), p. 23.

19. "Se destapan cartas sobre el cese al fuego," *El Espectador*, July 23, 2001; "Piden cese de hostilidades," *El Tiempo*, July 24, 2001.

20. From a written statement issued on May 15, 2001, from the Displaced Community of Upper and Lower Naya, titled "A la opinión pública nacional y mundial: Orígenes y consecuencias de la massacre paramilitary en el Naya," distributed to local and national journalists.

21. Human Rights Watch, *The Sixth Division*.

22. From author interviews with survivors of the Naya massacre who chose not to be identified, conducted in Caloto, Cauca, during the Extraordinary Indigenous Congress of the Regional Indigenous Council of Cauca, CRIC, August 18, 2001.

23. Castaño, Carlos, "La Operación Antisubversiva del Naya," *Editorial Semanal de las AUC*, April 23, 2001. This is available at http://www.colombialibre.org/editori/crecenauc.htm .

24. From author interviews with eyewitnesses.

25. Human Rights Watch, *The Sixth Division*.

26. See Murillo, M., "Mitos de la guerra contra las drogas en Colombia," *El Diario/La Prensa*, February 7, 2000.

27. Aranguren Molina, M., *Mi Confesión: Carlos Castaño revela sus secretos* (Bogotá: Editorial Oveja Negra, 2001).

28. Romero, *Paramilitares y autodefensas: 1982–2003*, pp. 30–31.

29. Restrepo, "The Equivocal Dimensions of Human Rights," p. 103.

30. Richani, N., "Colombia at the Crossroads: The Future of the Peace Accords," *NACLA Report on the Americas*, XXXV, No. 4, January/February 2002.

31. Cubides, "From Private to Public Violence," pp. 144–145.

32. "Mano dura o tenaza paramilitar? Por que en Antióquia el modelo predicado por Uribe Vélez no es tan bueno como lo pintan?" *Alternativa*, December 1996, No. 5.

33. "Los diálogos con el paramilitarismo: ¿Paz o impunidad? *Desde Abajo*, June 15–July 15, 2003, p. 6.

34. Some people estimate the percentage to be even greater, with two independent Congress members telling me recently that at least half of the House and Senate was controlled by AUC sympathizers, making it very difficult to function as an aggressive political opposition within the legislature.

35. Green, E., "Justice Department Indicts Colombian AUC Leaders on Drug Charges—Will Seek Extradition of Members of Paramilitary Group to U.S.," *The Washington File* (Washington, DC: Office of International Information Programs, U.S. Department of State, September 24, 2002); see also "Estados Unidos pide a jefe paramilitar Carlos Castaño en extradición por narcotráfico," *El Tiempo*, September 24, 2002.

36. On May 4, 2003, Alex Lee, chief political officer at the U.S. Embassy in Bogotá, and Stewart Tuttle, the head of the embassy's human rights division, met with representatives of the AUC, a meeting that caused a bit of a stir in the Colombian press at the time. State Department officials, who describe the paramilitaries as an international terrorist organization, claimed the meeting was meant to reiterate Washington's extradition demand for Castaño and Mancuso, while an AUC spokesperson said it was called to see if some kind of amnesty could be arranged for the paramilitary chiefs. Regardless of the nature of the meeting, it called into question the Bush administration's ongoing mantra that "we don't negotiate with terrorists." It was consistent, however, with President Uribe's outreach to the paramilitary leadership. See Donahue, S., "Bush and the Paramilitaries," *CounterPunch*, retrieved from http://www.counterpunch.org/donahue07102003.html on July 18, 2003.

37. Selsky, A., "Colombia Ready for Talks with Rebel Group," Associated Press, January 8, 2003.

38. As I pointed out in chapter 3, the secretariat of the FARC had insisted throughout the failed peace process with Pastrana that the government had to put an

end to paramilitary terror and break the links between the army and the AUC in order to move the process forward. This was not done, and it turned out to be one of the causes of the breakdown in talks. Naturally, the AUC could not make the same kinds of demands on the government of Uribe, given the different set of circumstances, namely that the guerrillas were fighting both the government and the AUC. Nevertheless, in the initial stages of talks between Uribe and the paramilitaries, tensions arose about how to deal with the guerrillas once the AUC demobilized. As it turns out, Castaño and Mancuso were eventually convinced that Uribe's stepped-up war against the FARC and ELN would yield results quickly, thus lessening the need for the AUC's "illegitimate" war machine. See "Un buen comienzo," *Semana*, July 21, 2003, no. 1,107, pp. 32–35.

39. The document in question was entitled "Las Autodefensas Unidas de Colombia, AUC, desde la perspectiva jurídica" (The United Self-Defense Groups of Colombia, AUC, from the Legal Perspective). It was drawn up by three high-profile lawyers from Colombia who in the past had defended narcotraffickers, ex-paramilitaries, and guerrillas in criminal cases, and who had been involved in talks between U.S. authorities and other narcotraffickers in the past. These lawyers met with the AUC leadership to come up with a comprehensive set of legal arguments that would provide the basis for the group to negotiate a demobilization agreement with the government without having to be concerned about the extradition requests pending on their heads. Ultimately, the goal of the proposal was to promote a bill in the Colombian Congress that would provide some legal protections to the demobilized paramilitaries. Among their primary points was that the crimes committed by the AUC were political in nature, that their decision to take up arms in defense of the state should be considered sedition but not terrorism, and that they were not armies that carry out private justice. Among the most controversial parts of the sixty-two-page document is the AUC's attempt to justify its financing through narcotrafficking. According to the legal arguments, their involvement in the drug trade was the only possible way to confront the "brutal attacks of the FARC and ELN . . . financed by incalculable sums of money through the trafficking in drugs, kidnapping, and extortion." As the document clearly points out, "revolution and counterinsurgency is not financed with medals, rosary beads, raffles, or the sale of beef patties." See "La Propuesta de las AUC," *Cambio*, July 7, 2003, No. 523, pp. 16–20.

40. "La Propuesta de las AUC," p. 19.

41. Sierra, L. M., and Mercado, B., "Seis retos con los 'paras'," *El Tiempo*, July 20, 2003, pp. 1–2.

42. This was expressed by many commentators and activists prior to and in the immediate aftermath of the July 2003 announcement that demobilization talks were moving forward between Uribe and the AUC. For example, in an open let-

ter to High Commissioner for Peace Luis Carlos Restrepo, Ivan Cepeda Castro, son of the late Senator Manuel Cepeda Vargas, who had been murdered by paramilitary hit men in the early 1990s, wrote that the murder of his father under the orders of Castaño himself must not go unpunished (as transmitted through Equipo Nizkor, Derechos Humanos de SERPAJ, January 20, 2003). See also Colombia Nunca Más, "Los diálogos con el paramilitarismo: ¿Paz o impunidad?" *Desde Abajo*, June 15–July 15, 2003, pp. 6–8.

43.   Entrevista Real de Yamid, "Habla Mancuso," *El Tiempo*, July 20, 2003, p. 21.

44.   This position was expressed by several columnists in news magazines and newspapers, but in hard news accounts of the preliminary AUC-government demobilization agreement it was scarcely mentioned. See Petro, G., "De paradojas y paramilitares," *El Espectador*, July 20, 2003, p. 16-A; Caballero, A., "No hay peor sordo . . . ," *Semana*, July 21–28, 2003, p. 102.

45.   Based on author interviews with members of the Cauca departmental assembly and the governor's office who asked not to be identified, January 2003.

46.   Burger, K., "U.S. Special Forces Give Colombians Anti-Terrorism Training," *Jane's Defence Weekly*, January 8, 2003.

47.   "Habla Mancuso," *El Tiempo*.

Chapter 5: National Security, Dependency, and Exploitation

1.   Caballero, A., "Los responsables del desastre (Parábola del bus)," in *Quiénes nos tienen Jodidos* (Bogotá: Editorial Oveja Negra, 2002), pp. 16–17.

2.   Bushnell, D., *The Making of Modern Colombia: A Nation in Spite of Itself* (Berkeley: University of California Press, 2001), p. 213.

3.   Page, S., "Sununu: Bush Would Send Troops," *Newsday*, September 4, 1989, p. 18.

4.   Treaster, J., "U.S. Sending Wrong Equipment to Fight Drugs, Colombians Say," *New York Times*, September 12, 1989, p. A5. For a detailed description of how this early period of Bush's war on drugs in Colombia evolved, see Chomsky, N., *Deterring Democracy* (New York: Hill and Wang, 1992), pp. 114–121.

5.   "Colombia recibirá 100 millones de dólares de E.U. como premio por apoyar guerra en Irak," March 23, 2003; retrieved from http://eltiempo.terra.com.co/coar/noticias/ARTICULO-WEB-NOTA_INTERIOR-1032882.html on March 24, 2003.

6.   Molano, A., "La Paz en su Laberinto," in *Qué Está Pasando en Colombia?: Anatomía de un País en Crísis* (Bogotá: El Ancora Editores, 2001), p. 103.

7.   "El Campo se sembró de pobres," *El Tiempo*, August 5, 2001, p. 1D.

8. Marx, G., "Coffee Crisis Ravages Colombia: Falling Prices Fuel Coca Production and Civil War," *Chicago Tribune*, April 20, 2003; retrieved from http://www.chicagotribune.com/news/nationworld/chi-0304 200431apr20,1,2241910.story on April 21, 2003.

9. Edwards, B., "Privatization in Colombia: Corruption and Waste, Unemployment and Poverty," *Colombia Update*, 14:1 (Washington, DC: Colombia Human Rights Network, 2002).

10. By 2003, things changed only in that military spending became the top priority of the Uribe government, again with the Colombian worker forced to foot the bill in terms of cuts in salaries, benefits, and services. The president's "reforms" opened up the national budget for a vast increase in military expenditures, including a measure reducing all public-sector salaries by 30 percent. He pushed through a reduction in overnight and overtime wages and an increase of the retirement age. The political referendum he promoted throughout the first year of his administration included a number of regressive measures affecting workers, including a two-year freeze on the salaries of those who received double the minimum wage. Most controversial was the complete restructuring of *Telecom* and *Ecopetrol*, the state telecommunications and oil companies, respectively. These actions were made possible under law 489 of 2002, which gave President Uribe extraordinary powers to reform, adjust, transform, or liquidate all state enterprises. One of the direct results has been to completely deunionize both entities, ostensibly in the name of modernization and efficiency. The long-term impact of all these measures on workers was criticized by many analysts who predicted further social decay and polarization. This opinion was shared by even those who otherwise welcomed his security strategy. See Ahumada, C., "Una Decada en Reversa," in *Qué Está Pasando en Colombia: Anatomía de un País en Crísis* (Bogotá: El Ancora Editores, 2001), p. 18; "Privatización diferida: Telecom," *Desde Abajo*, June 15–July 15, 2003, p. 8; "La joya de la corona," *Cambio*, June 23, 2003, pp. 26–28; "El hueco social," *El Tiempo*, August 7, 2003, pp. 1-12.

11. "Avanza el proceso de unidad CUT-CTC," *Política Educativa: Informativo de la Central Unitaria de Trabajadores-CUT*, May–June 2001, No. 3.

12. From the document "Memorias: Prevención, protección, y acción por los derechos civíles y políticos," published by the CUT's Department of Human Rights, Bogotá, November 2000, p. 5.

13. "Colombian Trade Unionists Face Daunting Difficulties," *Colombia Update*, 14:1 (Washington, DC: Colombia Human Rights Network, 2002).

14. Sixel, L. M., "Union to protest at Coke Annual Meeting," *Houston Chronicle*, April 15, 2003; "Campaña mundial contra Coca Cola: La chispa de la muerte," *Desde Abajo*, July 15–August 15, 2003, p. 15.

15. Dudley, S., and Murillo, M., "Oil in a Time of War," *NACLA Report on the Americas*, 31: 5, March/April 1998, pp. 42–46.

16. For a comprehensive analysis of the economic and political implications of *Plan Colombia*, see Estrada Alvarez, J., ed., *Plan Colombia: Ensayos Críticos* (Bogotá: Universidad Nacional de Colombia—Facultad de Derecho, Ciencias Políticas y Sociales, 2001).

17. See Organización Nacional Indígena de Colombia (ONIC), *Tierra Profanada: Grandes Proyectos en Territorios Indígenas en Colombia* (Bogotá: ONIC/ Disloque Editores, 1995).

18. Klare, M., "Detrás del petróleo colombiano: intenciones ocultas," Agencia Latinoamericana de Información, cited in Estrada Alvarez, *Plan Colombia: Ensayos Críticos*, p. 52.

19. Roldan, R., "Aproximación histórica a la explotación de petroleo en territoriás indígenas," in ONIC, *Tierra Profanada*, pp. 267–268.

20. Ibid., p. 270.

21. Dudley, S., and Murillo, M., "The U'Wa Struggle to Survive," *NACLA Report on the Americas*, 31: 5, March–April 1998, p. 45.

22. For one detailed analysis, see Vargas, R., "Failures of the Anti-Narcotics Policy: Fumigation and Interdiction at the Source," *Voices from Colombia*, winter 2001–2002 (Colombia Media Project, New York; colmediaproject@aol.com).

23. Isacson, A., "Colombia Peace in Tatters," *NACLA Report on the Americas*, 35: 5, March–April 2002; see also Center for International Policy (CIP), "The 2003 Aid Request," http://www.ciponline.org/Colombia/aid03.htm . Meanwhile, for fiscal year 2004, the U.S. Congress approved $574 million in aid, of which $427 million was destined for the fumigation program, training, and the creation of mobile brigades, and $150 million was destined for alternative development, strengthening of the judicial system, and aid for the displaced.

24. From "Globalization and 'Free' Trade in Colombia," *A Report by the Information Network of the Americas (INOTA)*, retrieved from http://www.colombiareport.org/globalization_colombia.htm on January 21, 2003.

25. Isacson, A., "Colombia Peace in Tatters"; citing A. Barrionuevo and T. Herrick, "The Threat of Terror Abroad Isn't New for Companies Like Occidental," *Wall Street Journal*, February 5, 2002.

26. Forero, J., "New Role for U.S. in Colombia: Protecting a Vital Oil Pipeline," *New York Times*, October 4, 2002, p. A1.

27. "Corte de cuentas: Los ases del orden público," *El Tiempo*, July 27, 2003, pp. 1–7.

28. De Cordoba, J., "Tense Borders, Ad Hoc Militias, U.S. Special Forces: It's Colombia," *Wall Street Journal*, April 11, 2003, p. A9.

29. Rueda G., C. I., "E.U. cuidara intereses petroleros en Colombia, dice embajadora," *El Tiempo*, February 10, 2002.

30. The actual quantity of U.S. forces deployed in Colombia is difficult to measure. When *Plan Colombia* was implemented, Congress established a limit of 500 U.S. military personnel and 300 civilian contractors at any given time. These self-designated "temporary" forces are ostensibly involved in a broad array of functions, both civil and military, ranging from combat training, air support, and equipment maintenance, to infrastructure development, "human rights" training, and humanitarian assistance. In 2002, for example, according to the State Department, U.S. military forces in Colombia trained 6,477 Colombian soldiers, while in the first half of 2003 another 2,800 were trained, of whom 655 were specifically for counterinsurgency purposes. With the deployment of the 150-person U.S. special forces contingent in February 2003, however, not only did the total number of U.S. military personnel surpass the congressionally mandated limit, but also for the first time they were explicitly permitted to engage in direct combat with "enemy" forces. See "Presencia de militares estadounidenses en Colombia: Inmoral e ilegal," *Desde Abajo*, July 15–August 15, 2003, p. 3; Gómez Maseri, S., "Colombia, prioridad en entrenamiento de E.U.," *El Tiempo*, July 29, 2003, pp. 1-5.

31. Arrington, V., "U.S. Lawmakers Threaten Retaliation Against Rebels Believed to Be Holding Three Americans Captive," Associated Press, February 20, 2003.

32. "Presencia de militares estadounidenses en Colombia."

33. "Fumigation Continues Amidst Widespread Killings in Putumayo," *Colombia Update*, 14:1 (Washington, DC: Colombia Human Rights Network, 2002).

34. From testimonials by Eder Jair Sánchez, member of the departmental assembly of Putumayo and representative of ANUC, the National Association of Peasant Farmers; and Gloria Flores, coordinator of the human rights program of MINGA Association, a Bogotá-based NGO working closely with peasants farmers in the department of Putumayo; September 26–27, 2002, at a conference sponsored by the Colombia Media Project, at Hunter College, New York City.

35. From a press release issued on March 7, 2002, by the Office of National Drug Control Policy, Washington, DC; reported in Gedda, G., "Bush Dismayed by Coca Production," Associated Press, March 8, 2002; and "U.S. Sees 25 Percent Surge in Coca Crops in Colombia," Reuters, March 7, 2002; also, Marquis, C., "White House Reports a Decline in Colombia's Coca Cultivation," *New York Times*, February 28, 2003, p. A5.

36. Gómez Maseri, S., "Cultivos de coca se desplazan a fronteras," *El Tiempo*, July 30, 2003, pp. 1-7.

37. "Colombia Ratifies International Criminal Court, but War Crimes OK for 7 Years," *Colombia Update*, 14:1 (Washington, DC: Colombia Human Rights Network, 2002).

38. See House Resolution H-358, "Expressing Support for Democratically Elected Government of Colombia and Its Efforts to Counter Threats from U.S.-Designated Foreign Terrorist Organizations," March 6, 2002; Human Rights Watch, *The Sixth Division: Military-Paramilitary Ties and U.S. Policy in Colombia*, September 2001.

39. Carrigan, A., "War or Peace? Colombia's New President Must Choose Between Washington and His Own People," *In These Times*, August 7, 2002.

40. Pizarro, E., "Terrorismo y democracia: el caso de Colombia," in *Terrorismo y Seguridad* (Bogotá: Planeta/Semana, 2003), p. 67.

41. "Elogios para Uribe," *El Tiempo*, August 8, 2003, p. 1-3.

42. Quoting Marc Grossman, Undersecretary of State for Political Affairs, in a visit to Colombia in late July 2003, *El Tiempo*, July 31, 2003, p. 1-4.

43. As reported in "Plan Colombia obtiene la peor calificación: De ONGs y legisladores demócratas," *El Heraldo*, July 11, 2003, p. 9-A. For more details, visit http://www.wola.org/ and http://www.lawg.org/ .

Chapter 6: Colombia in the News

1. For this study, a search on the LexisNexis service for the terms *Colombia* and *terrorism* in the headlines and lead paragraphs of stories published during the year following September 11, 2001, was carried out between October 14, 2002, and December 1, 2002. The search yielded a total of 118 articles.

2. While numerous media scholars have written about this tendency on the part of U.S. journalists, I especially like Jamieson, K. H. and Campbell, K. K., *The Interplay of Influence: News, Advertising, Politics, and the Mass Media*, 5th ed. (New York: Wadsworth, 2001), pp. 40–81.

3. Marquis, C., "U.S. Supports Colombian on Ultimatum to Rebels," *New York Times*, January 11, 2002.

4. Gedda, G., "House Wants Ideas to Help Colombia," Associated Press, March 7, 2002.

5. "The War in Colombia Intensifies," *New York Times*, editorial, March 9, 2002.

6. "Remember Colombia," *Washington Post*, editorial, January 14, 2002.

7. "Colombia's War: Bush, Congress Should Consider Military Aid," *Dallas Morning News*, February 27, 2002; "Survival Now Threatened," *South Florida Sun-Sentinel*, editorial, February 27, 2002; "Colombia at War," *Washington Times*, editorial, February 28, 2002.

8. Marquis, C., "U.S. Supports Colombia on Ultimatum to Rebels," *New York Times*, January 11, 2002.

9. DeYoung, K., "Lawmakers Dispute Report Linking IRA, Colombia Guerrillas; Some Wary of Counter-Terrorism Plan," *Washington Post*, April 25, 2002.

10. DeYoung, K., "U.S. Certifies Colombia on Rights," *Washington Post*, May 2, 2002.

11. Marquis, C., "U.S. to Explore Aid to Colombia, Citing Threat of Terrorism" *New York Times*, March 3, 2002.

12. Several examples of this attitude can be found in Santos, A., ed., *Terrorismo y Seguridad* (Bogotá: Planeta/Semana, 2003). One of the most extreme examples of deliberately neglecting history as a potential cause of the current crisis is written by conservative writer and diplomat P. A. Mendoza, "Las FARC: Un enclave terrorista en Colombia," pp. 193–210.

13. Forero, J., "After a Killing, Colombian Leader Has to Decide on Peace Talks," *New York Times*, October 5, 2001.

14. Molano, A., "Prensa Libre," *Contravía: Textos para un Debate*, No. 9 (Bogotá, Colombia, 2002).

15. "State of Commotion," *The Economist*, August 17, 2002.

16. Wilson, S., "Colombia Elects a Hard Liner on Fighting Rebels," *Washington Post*, May 27, 2002.

17. Ibid.

18. Lipton, E., "Cold Numbers: A Census of the Sept. 11 Victims," *New York Times*, April 19, 2002.

19. Ojito, M., "A Familiar Anguish Revisited," *New York Times*, September 24, 2001.

20. Barringer, F., "New Tactic of Terrorists Is to Attack the Media," *New York Times*, October 15, 2001.

21. Contreras, J., "A Little Vietnam," *Newsweek*, June 24, 2002.

22. "Help for Colombia," *Washington Post*, editorial, February 24, 2002.

23. Milligan, S., "New England Lawmakers Sharpen Focus on Latin America," *Boston Globe*, June 16, 2002.

24. For detailed definitions about terrorism, see Pizarro, E., in Santos, A., ed., *Terrorismo y Seguridad*, pp. 27–70.

25. DeYoung, K., "Hill Stance on Colombia Aid Shifts; Bush Officials Seek More Funds for Counterterrorism," *Washington Post*, March 4, 2002.

26. DeYoung, K., "Colombia to Get Aid in Fighting Insurgents; U.S. Will Increase Intelligence Sharing," *Washington Post*, February 22, 2002.

27. Selsky, A., "Colombia Ready for Talks With Rebel Group," Associated Press, January 8, 2003; although this was not part of the sample, it should be considered significant considering the fact that the FARC and ELN were (and are) nowhere near the negotiating table. Throughout 2003, however, as talks unfolded between the government and the AUC, the term "rebels" was used repeatedly in the U.S. news media to describe the paramilitaries.

28. Weiner, T., "U.S. Official Predicts Drop in Colombian Cocaine," *New York Times*, February 22, 2002.

29. Bender, B., "Fighting Terror, Perceiving a Wider Threat, Political Strategy: U.S. Finds a Palatable Word for Military Aid to Colombia; Scant Proof Found of Any Terror Links," *Boston Globe*, May 5, 2002.

30. Ibid.

31. "Remember Colombia," *Washington Post*.

32. Quoted from Peter Romero, assistant secretary of state for the Western Hemisphere in the Clinton administration, "Save Colombia," *Washington Post*, February 20, 2002.

33. Ibid.

34. Bender, B., "Fighting Terror Global Operations; Terror War Remaps Troop Deployments," *Boston Globe*, January 17, 2002.

35. Gans, H., *Democracy and the News* (New York: Oxford University Press, 2003), p. 70.

36. To be fair, there does exist a limited tradition of truly independent journalism in Colombia. Over the years, the press has echoed the denunciations of human rights groups and published reports about corrupt military and political officials. But for the most part, the Colombian news media tend to grasp and expose primarily the outrages committed against certain types of Colombians, disregarding the rights of thousands of ordinary citizens. This should come as no surprise if one considers the ownership patterns of the press, radio, and television in Colombia, which reads like a who's who of the dominant family names in politics and business, including a number of former presidents. The current vice president comes from the family that owns the nation's largest newspaper, *El Tiempo*. Naturally, a systematic monitoring and analysis of the Colombian media would be needed to illustrate how these structures affect content, and in turn political culture, studies that have been conducted inside Colombia over the years. Nevertheless, it would not be a

stretch to argue that the highly concentrated nature of Colombia's mass media system is a significant mechanism used by the political and economic elite to maintain its grip on power.

Chapter 7: Conclusion

1. For two very good texts, see Archila, M., Delgado A., García, M., and Prada, E., *25 Años de luchas sociales en Colombia: 1975–2000* (Bogotá: CINEP, 2002); Archila, M., and Pardo, M., eds., *Movimientos sociales, estado y democracia en Colombia* (Bogotá: Centro de Estudios Sociales, Universidad Nacional de Colombia, 2001).

2. Romero, M., *Paramilitares y autodefensas: 1982–2003* (Bogotá: Instituto de Estudios Políticos y Relaciones Internacionales, Universidad Nacional de Colombia, 2003), p. 39.

3. From a letter to President Alvaro Uribe Vélez, from José Miguel Vivanco, Human Rights Watch, April 21, 2003; retrieved from http://www.hrw.org/press/2003/04/colombia042103ltr.htm on May 3, 2003.

4. Ibid.

5. Various authors, *El embrujo autoritario, Primer año de Álvaro Uribe Vélez* (Bogotá: Ediciones Antropos, 2003); retrieved from http://www.viaalterna.com.co/pembrujo.htm on October 13, 2003.

6. Center for International Policy, Project on Colombia, "The Uribe Government and NGOs," September 8, 2003; retrieved from http://www.ciponline.org/colombia/ngos.htm on October 13, 2003.

7. From the written statement by the above-mentioned writers, presented at the XIII International Forum of Poetry and Peace for Colombia, held in Medellín, July 2003, and provided to the author by Arturo Alape.

Index

About the Author

MARIO ALFONSO MURILLO is an assistant professor in the School of Communication at Hofstra University in Hempstead, New York, and teaches media studies courses at New York University. A veteran radio journalist, he has reported and produced award-winning programs and documentaries for a number of broadcast outlets, including WBAI, the Pacifica Radio Network, and National Public Radio. He is the author of *Islands of Resistance: Puerto Rico, Vieques, and U.S. Policy*, published by Seven Stories Press in 2001. He resides in Brooklyn, New York.

JESUS REY AVIRAMA is a founding member and former president of the Regional Indigenous Council of Cauca, CRIC, the oldest and largest Indigenous organization in Colombia. A member of the Kokonuco people, Rey Avirama has been a direct participant in the struggle for the land, cultural, economic, and civil rights of Colombia's indigenous and peasant communities for more than thirty years.